# THE FRAGRANCE OF RAIN

This title is part of a series of books entitled
ESSENTIAL INDIA EDITIONS.
Each book in the series will explore a foundational aspect of the country in new and thought-provoking ways.

ALSO IN THIS SERIES

*Our Living Constitution: A Concise Introduction & Commentary*
by Shashi Tharoor

*Language of the Immortals: A Concise Study of Sanskrit*
by G. N. Devy

*Song of India: A Study of the National Anthem*
by Rudrangshu Mukherjee

*Dance of Freedom: A Short History of Bharata Natyam*
by Leela Samson

*The Mysterious World of Tigers: A Book of Discovery*
by Valmik Thapar

*The Sari Eternal: A Tribute*
by Lakshmi Puri

*The Social Life of Indian Trains: A Journey*
by Amitava Kumar

*The Ghosts of Indian Small Towns: A Journey Through Time*
by Ruskin Bond

*Flower of India: Ways of Seeing the Lotus*
by Devdutt Pattanaik

*Do You Know Your Hinduism?: Notes for Modern-day Hindus*
by Rajmohan Gandhi

# THE FRAGRANCE OF RAIN

## A BRIEF HISTORY OF THE MONSOON

Stephen Alter

ALEPH

ALEPH

ALEPH BOOK COMPANY
An independent publishing firm
promoted by ***Rupa Publications India***

First published in India in 2026
by Aleph Book Company
161-B/4, Gulmohar House,
Yusuf Sarai Community Centre,
New Delhi 110049



ISBN: 978-93-6523-030-7

1 3 5 7 9 10 8 6 4 2

Printed in India.

For Renu and Akshay

मेघैर्व्योम नवाम्बुभिर्वसुमती विद्युल्लताभिर्दिशो
धाराभिर्गगनं वनानि कुटजैः पूरैर्वृता निम्नगाः ।
एकां घातयितुं वियोगविधुरां दीनां वराकीं स्त्रियं
प्रावृट्काल हतश वर्णय कृतं मिथ्या किमाडम्बरम् ॥

The heavens
with clouds
the land with fast running water

the horizon with lightning jags,
torrents of rain

Milky kutaja petals
stroke the forests
creeks churn through the foothills –

Why expose a lone woman
to such pageant

O season of rain

the torment
the sweet bitter need to be

touched.

—Vidya (approx. seventh-ninth century CE)
Translated from the Sanskrit by Andrew Schelling

# CONTENTS

# 1

# PETRICHOR

Early one morning, towards the end of May 2025, I woke up to the sound of distant thunder. Stepping outside in the first light before dawn, I could see that the sky above me was a pale blue, but off in the distance, beyond the Shivalik Hills on the other side of the Doon Valley, layers of dark clouds smeared the horizon. A light but steady breeze was blowing in my face and the trees around me swayed and trembled. Within twenty minutes, the advancing storm had crossed the Shivalik Range, like a shadowy wave breaking over a reef. Bright streaks of lightning lanced the bruised and swollen clouds while the thunder grew louder. Instead of a far-off rumble, it now boomed and crackled.

On many occasions, I have watched the

monsoon arrive in Mussoorie, though it often ambushes us when least expected. A dark tide of cumulonimbus formations, with towering thunderheads, appear over the plains, bearing down on the mountains with relentless momentum. Some of these clouds have travelled the length of India from the southern coast of Kerala, passing over the Western Ghats and the Deccan Plateau before flying above the Satpura, Vindhya, and Aravalli ranges, as well as the Gangetic Plain. The land beneath them has been heated by the summer sun, which contributes to the rising air and condensation. Along the way, a few rain showers occur but it is only when the clouds collide with the Himalaya that they release most of their precipitation.

As the warm, humid winds approach the mountains, they come in contact with colder temperatures and the air currents are disrupted. Turbulent updrafts carry tiny droplets of water high into the clouds where they freeze and form hail. These pellets of ice are spun violently round and round by swirling winds.

As the hailstones accumulate more and more moisture, they grow larger and heavier until they fall to earth. Meanwhile, as the ice crystals rub together within the clouds, their friction generates positive and negative charges of static electricity that ignite bolts of lightning, which are accompanied by loud thunderclaps when superheated air suddenly expands.

Over the years, we have lost several trees on our property to lightning strikes. One of the oldest deodars at Oakville, which was probably planted when the house was first built in the 1840s, stood more than 40 metres tall. During a powerful pre-monsoon storm, in 2020, it was destroyed by a bolt of lightning that split the trunk down the middle and scattered splinters of wood, some as small as toothpicks, in all directions. Another deodar, which had strands of barbed wire nailed to it, as a fence to keep out stray cattle, was hit the next year. An electric charge travelled through the wire and shattered a gate post to which it was attached. Both strikes landed frighteningly close to our house and the explosions sounded like bombs going off.

Standing at the edge of our yard at Oakville, as the storm closed in on the mountains, I could feel the energy and tension in the air. The wind grew stronger and rougher, buffeting the deodar trees overhead while the imminent dawn retreated back into darkness. A flash of lightning to the east was followed, almost immediately, by a blast of thunder. Moments later, another lightning bolt tore through the gloom and struck a ridge below. The detonation shook the ground beneath my feet as hailstones, the size of chickpeas, began to pelt the flower beds behind me. One hit my head, and another ricocheted off my arm. Turning, I ran towards the house and pushed my way through the kitchen door. At that same moment, the electricity went off as another flash of lightning struck somewhere on the hill above. By now the hail was rattling on the sheet metal roof, as if tonnes of gravel were pouring from the sky.

After unplugging my laptop and other appliances, in case the lightning travelled through the wires, I stood at the window of my study and watched the storm. The yard was now white with hail, which battered the oak trees, shredding leaves and breaking twigs, as the wind grappled with their branches. Thirty minutes earlier, the morning had been calm, with only a distant hint of turbulent weather, but now we were inside a maelstrom as churning clouds washed over the mountains like an airborne tsunami.

The hail continued for ten minutes and then tapered off into rain while the lightning and thunder moved away to the north. As the wind continued to wrestle with the trees, the clouds shed their moisture in a deluge that persisted for another half hour before the storm eased. The lights in our house finally came back on and the drumming of rain on the roof fell silent, except for a few stray drops from the trees.

Stepping outside again, I could see coils

of mist unfurling up the slope of the ridge, hiding and exposing the trees. Everything was drenched, from the grass under my shoes to the spongy bark on rhododendron trees, as well as the dripping leaves of a Himalayan maple that stands taller than the house. However, what struck me most of all was the smell that lingers after a storm. It is an odour I know well but every time it fills the air, this natural fragrance takes me by surprise. A sweet, slightly musky odour, fresh, yet with a hint of decomposing leaves, it had a sensual, alluring perfume.

Urdu and Hindi poets refer to this earthy aroma as 'sondhi mahak' (sweet scent) or 'baarish ki khushboo' (the fragrance of rain) which evokes romantic connotations at the beginning of the monsoon. For generations, perfumers in Kannauj, an ancient city in Uttar Pradesh, have extracted similar smells from dried clay through steam distillation. The bottled essence, mixed with sandalwood oil, is known as 'mitti attar' (earth perfume).

In 1964, two Australian chemists, Isabel Bear and Richard Thomas, learned about mitti attar and undertook a series of experiments which revealed that the scent emanates not only from soil but also from rocks. After analysing the chemistry of certain stones, which were dried and baked, they used steam and solvents to release aerosols. Ultimately, the chemists determined that the fragrance which accompanies the rain, particularly after a period of dry weather, comes from a combination of mineral compounds in the rocks, as well as residual oils absorbed from plant leaves and other organic matter. Bear and Thomas named this odour 'petrichor', which derives from the Greek 'petri' for rocks and 'ichor', the mythological blood of the gods.

Petrichor is not a single, isolated smell but varies according to the geology and ecology of each region. In Mussoorie, one of the distinctive elements is the tang of dry oak leaves infused by the rain as well as the chalky scent of limestone in these hills. Scientists have also determined that another contributing factor is the powerful force of lightning strikes that split oxygen molecules to create ozone, which has a sharp, 'clean' odour.

This sudden, violent hailstorm and the familiar smell in its aftermath, suggested that the monsoon had begun, though I couldn't be sure. Earlier, during the middle of May, a series of heavy downpours struck Mussoorie, and people were convinced that the monsoon had arrived sooner than expected. Landslides blocked roads and several hillside houses were threatened, the unstable mountain slopes sloughing off beneath precarious foundations and retaining walls.

However, after a week of tempestuous storms, the rain stopped as abruptly as it began. For the next few days, we had bright sunshine every morning, though clouds swept in around midday and by late afternoon our family home was cloaked in an opaque shroud of mist. Situated at the eastern end of Landour ridge, Oakville is one of the first houses to be enveloped by ascending rafts of water vapour that are carried uphill on anabatic winds, which rise as the air grows warmer. In the evening, when the air cools, katabatic winds reverse the flow, and the clouds descend to lower elevations. Also known as 'gravity winds', these thermal currents are a key climatic feature of the Himalayan foothills.

Years ago, when I was growing up in Mussoorie, we used to speak about the 'choti barsaat', or the small monsoon, which sometimes preceded the main event by a couple of weeks. Between these first rainstorms in May and the full onslaught of the monsoon, which generally commenced by mid-June, there was often a brief hiatus of ten to fifteen days. But our collective memories are short, especially when it comes to the weather. Nowadays, every time an unexpected storm occurs, people shake their heads and despair about 'climate change'. What they often forget is that the weather in Mussoorie has always been erratic at this time of year. The accelerated warming of our planet is very real and alarming, as are the rising levels of greenhouse gases in the atmosphere, particularly carbon dioxide emissions from power plants, factories, and motor vehicles. At the same time, we must recognize that the true consequences of climate change will be far more profound and prolonged than these intermittent pre-monsoon squalls that have been occurring over millions of years.

For another week, after the sudden hailstorm, our mornings continued to be clear. From the crest of the ridge above Oakville, I could see the snow peaks of Garhwal to the north before the clouds drifted in and erased my view. The forests were no longer dry, as they were in April and early May—no danger of wildfires, though the monsoon foliage had yet to break forth and the fallen oak leaves on the paths remained brittle underfoot.

Then, on 26 May, weather reports in the newspapers announced that an 'active Madden–Julian Oscillation (MJO)...a complex, moving system of winds, clouds and pressure (that) originates in the Indian Ocean', and heralds the monsoon, was approaching Kerala, 2,500 kilometres south of Mussoorie.

# 2

# AWAITING THE MONSOON

On 4 June, I flew to Kochi (formerly Cochin) hoping to see cloud banks massing offshore before they ploughed inland like an armada of moisture bombarding the Malabar Coast. But the sky was clear as we touched down at the airport. By the time I reached my hotel near the old Dutch cemetery, facing the Arabian Sea, nothing more than a few tattered scraps of cirrus hovered overhead. The only evidence of the monsoon was the humidity, thick and syrupy, as if the air were infused with warm palm sap.

Late in the afternoon, I set out for a walk along the seafront, where a desultory surf crashed against a wall of jumbled rocks. The pale sun drooped through a gauze-like haze that blurred the horizon and no breeze stirred off the water. Ice cream sellers were short of customers and most of the promenade was deserted at this time of day, as the temperature simmered in the upper thirties. Sweating and searching for shade at every step, I quickly retreated to my air-conditioned room where I consulted a folder of recent clippings from the *Indian Express*.

Over a week earlier, Anjali Marar in Bengaluru had reported that, 'The southwest monsoon arrived in Kerala on Saturday, eight days ahead of its normal date of arrival on June 1, according to the India Meteorological Department (IMD). This was the earliest onset of the monsoon over the Indian mainland since 2009, when it reached Kerala on May 23.'

The next day, Alind Chauhan in New Delhi assured his readers that, 'The India Meteorological Department (IMD) has forecast "above normal" rainfall—105% of the long period average (LPA)—during the June–September southwest monsoon season. The IMD said earlier this month that all major drivers of the Indian monsoon, such as El Niño Southern oscillation (ENSO) in the equatorial Pacific Ocean and the Indian Ocean Dipole (IOD), were favourable.'

The arrival of the monsoon in Kerala and its progress northwards across India is one of the most carefully watched climatic events on earth, though it often defies forecasts and predictions. While the monsoon seldom fails to materialize, except in years of devastating drought, there is something elusive and ambiguous about the annual winds that carry overstuffed clouds from the Indian Ocean to the south-western tip of the subcontinent.

In his breezy, engaging travelogue, *Chasing the Monsoon*, Alexander Frater, pursued the course of the rains after they arrived at Kovalam Beach near Thiruvananthapuram, Kerala, on 2 June 1987. He tracked the progress of the monsoon up the Malabar Coast and through the heartland of India to the northeastern town of Cherrapunji in Meghalaya, often referred to as the wettest place on earth. From the outset, Frater admits to a certain element of uncertainty while stalking the rain.

'The monsoon seemed to be on its way and my journey in its company could commence. The fact that it had finally made its move was one worry less, but new doubts began to assail me.... An eccentric monsoon, starting and stopping at whim, perhaps making unscheduled diversions, would make life very complicated.' Nevertheless, while standing on the beach with a crowd of revellers awaiting the first downpour, Frater felt the excitement and anticipation of the monsoon's arrival.

> The imbroglio of inky cloud swirling overhead contained nimbostratus, cumulonimbus and Lord knows what else; all riven by updraughts, downdraughts and vertical wind shear. Thunder boomed. Lightning went zapping into the sea, the leader stroke of one strike passing the ascending return stroke of the last so that

> the whole roaring edifice seemed supported on pillars of fire. Then, beyond the cumuliform anvils and soaring castellanus turrets, we saw a broad, ragged band of luminous indigo heading slowly inshore. Lesser clouds suspended beneath it like flapping curtains reached right down to the sea.

∽

The morning after my arrival in Kochi, I could see that it had rained during the night, though I'd been oblivious to it. The terrace outside my room was puddled with water and strewn with mango leaves from a tree that overshadowed the entrance to my hotel. A koel was calling somewhere close by but the storm had passed, and the sky was clear. Setting out for the sea wall again, I felt a hint of coolness in the air, though the humidity still clung to my skin. The graves of Dutch colonials were covered in green moss and overgrown with weeds and creepers. A locked gate kept intruders out of the cemetery but peering inside I could see the stolid masonry memorials packed together on sacred ground like crated cargo. Here sailors and merchants of the Dutch East India Company from the seventeenth- and eighteenth-century rest in peace within earshot of the pounding waves.

Around the corner lay a Beach Health Club, where energetic young men and a few middle-aged body builders were lifting weights under the spreading branches of an albizia, commonly known as a rain tree. Access to the seafront from this route was blocked by a sign that read 'No Entry', though a stream of morning walkers ignored the admonition. I followed them along an eroded embankment above a shallow cove and reached the paved seafront. This morning there was a breeze and it was pleasant walking under the peepul and banyan trees that grew along the sea wall. A young boy was flying a pink tissue paper kite while white-bellied sea eagles soared on the air currents just offshore. Parakeets were feasting on the spiral green pods of a jungle jalebi or monkeypod tree (*Pithecellobium dulce*), a South American species unintentionally brought to Asia aboard Spanish galleons.

Fort Kochi, as this part of town is officially known, was once the colonial quarter of Cochin. Originally built by the Portuguese with permission of the Raja of Cochin, it was named Fort Emmanuel. Overlooking the entrance to the harbour, the sea wall was guarded in succession by Portuguese, Dutch, and British cannons. One of these guns remained in place though its round muzzle had been painted red, which looked oddly like lipstick. Approaching the harbour was a cruise ship with six decks that pushed aside a wooden skiff manned by two fishermen, who paddled frantically through the wake. Stray dogs roamed the beach while the water, the colour of milky tea, was full of the broken stems and leaves of water hyacinths, another invasive species from South America that has colonized the lagoons and backwaters of Kerala, as well as other wetlands throughout India.

Dozens of purposeful young men in matching white t-shirts suddenly appeared, marching towards me, wearing rubber gloves and carrying plastic garbage bags. These volunteers quickly set to work picking up trash from the beach, which was littered with plastic flotsam. On a wall nearby, an artist had created two sets of angel's wings made from the discarded remains of rubber chappals retrieved from the sea. Their worn blue soles, arranged in an overlapping pattern, looked like bright feathers.

A line of Chinese fishing nets, for which Kochi is famous, punctuated the shore. Perched at the end of flimsy-looking jetties, these lift nets were cantilevered out over the water with counterweights to help hoist the catch. From a distance they resembled giant spider webs attached to slender ribs of bamboo. A short distance further on, I came upon a fish auction. A noisy cluster of thirty or forty buyers watched as each fisherman emptied his morning's catch on a white plastic tarpaulin, while the auctioneer rattled off bids. An assortment of different species from squid and prawns, to mullets and mackerel, were scooped up in plastic buckets by the fishmongers, who would take them to market and double the price. Nearby were a few stalls selling pomfret, kingfish, and barramundi. The fact that fishermen were still bringing in their catch meant that the monsoon had not started in earnest. When rough seas accompany the wind and rain, storm warnings are issued, and most smaller boats remain tied up on shore.

Later in the morning, I set out to explore Mattancherry, the historic commercial quarter of Kochi, which lies outside the walls of the fort, along the harbour. This includes 'Jew Town' where the old Paradesi Synagogue still stands at the end of a narrow lane hemmed in by souvenir shops. Though the exterior of the synagogue is modest, with a small clock tower, an opulent array of glass chandeliers is suspended from the ceiling inside and the floors are covered with antique Chinese tiles of blue and white. In the centre of the sanctuary stands an impressive brass bimah, or pulpit. There was once a thriving Jewish community in Kochi, made up of dispersed families that settled along the west coast of India, as early as two millennia ago. More recent Jewish traders came from Baghdad and other parts of the Middle East in the nineteenth century. All of these migrants were brought here by monsoon winds that carried them across the Arabian Sea.

Being a port city, Kochi has provided safe harbour for a variety of people from different regions of India and other parts of the world. Many of them came here to escape persecution such as the Hanafi Muslims from Kutch who built the oldest mosque still standing in Mattancherry, as well as Konkani Hindus who fled here after the Portuguese unleashed the inquisition in Goa. Among the many temples in Mattancherry, one of the most interesting is the Manja Bhagavathi shrine, where devotees present offerings of sea salt to the goddess. On the street outside is a pyramid of salt, over a metre high, sprinkled with peppercorns and turmeric. My autorickshaw driver told me that the shrine was built by Konkani refugees centuries ago.

Heading back to Fort Kochi, I stopped at the Indian Naval Maritime Museum, as much to find relief from the heat and humidity as to see the exhibits. Under the whirring ceiling fans, I browsed through a series of dioramas depicting Kochi's seafaring heritage. One display portrayed the arrival of Vasco da Gama, with a long beard and uncomfortably warm-looking admiral's coat and felt breeches. Next to him stood the mannequin of a Gujarati pilot, Kanji Malam, who guided the Portuguese fleet from the Maldives to Kerala, riding the trade winds of the monsoon.

As the first explorer to find a sea route from Europe to India, Vasco da Gama relied on the knowledge and experience of mariners from the Indian Ocean and Arabian Sea who knew these waters and winds. He made three voyages from Lisbon, around the Horn of Africa, to the Malabar Coast. Appointed viceroy of India, he finally died of malarial fever in Cochin on Christmas Eve, 1524. His body was initially buried in the Church of St. Francis, which lies within the fort, though da Gama's family later had his remains disinterred and shipped back to Portugal. The empty grave, covered by a plain stone slab, remains a hollow reminder of the tenuous fate of even the most intrepid voyagers.

Having missed my appointment with the monsoon in Kochi, I decided to drive up to Munnar—a hill station in the Western Ghats—125 kilometres inland from the coast. The rain clouds were likely to have retreated to the cooler elevation of the mountains, 1,600 metres above sea level. Manuel, my taxi driver, agreed that the monsoon was probably lurking somewhere in the highlands, as he drove us along a winding, two-lane road that passed through rubber plantations and pineapple farms.

After an hour and a half, the first foothills appeared, enormous protrusions of rock festooned with jungle. Beyond these lay the main bulwark of the Western Ghats, their uppermost ridges cloaked in mist. As we passed a large waterfall that spilled down a near-vertical granite slope, Manuel told me that when he drove by here three weeks ago, the falls had been dry. Because of recent rain, it was now in full flow. Several dozen tourist vehicles had stopped so their occupants could take selfies in front of the cascade, while vendors selling snacks had set up shop on both sides of the road. Falling water evokes a special fascination, perhaps because of its fluid force but also on account of its constantly changing shapes and patterns. In some ways, this is the purest form of motion, unconstrained and guided only by the invisible hand of gravity.

Munnar is well known for its tea gardens and as we approached the town many of the hillsides and plateaus were covered in a manicured mosaic of green bushes. Though *Camellia sinensis* is an invasive cultivar, which has overwhelmed much of the indigenous botany of this region, tea gardens have a deceptive, seemingly idyllic beauty. Here in the Western Ghats of Kerala, these plantations have replaced large swathes of grasslands that were once part of the original shola landscape. Typically, the rolling contours of South India's mountains were covered by open patches of veldt and scrubland that supported an extensive array of grasses, herbaceous plants, shrubs, and stunted trees. These were interspersed with dense stands of evergreen jungle, like seams of darker foliage growing in moist hollows and valleys. The same climate and terrain that supported the shola grasslands is ideal for growing tea, with an extended monsoon and a mix of sunshine and mist throughout the rest of the year.

The highest mountain in India, outside the Himalaya, is Anamudi peak, which rises above Munnar and stands at an altitude of 2,695 metres above sea level. Its name means the elephant's head and the bulky summit of grey granite resembles a tusker's looming profile. However, for most of my visit, Anamudi remained hidden in the clouds. Though I'd hoped to trek to the top of this mountain, there wasn't enough time to get the requisite permits and I had to content myself with a visit to Eravikulam National Park, which encircles the peak at elevations above 2,000 metres. This was once a private hunting preserve for tea planters in Munnar but became Kerala's first national park in 1978.

Eravikulam is efficiently organized with forest department buses that carried us above the tea gardens into a restricted tourist zone, with short walking trails. Surrounded by clouds, I finally felt as if I were in the presence of the monsoon, though there was little rain and hardly any wind. Dozens of waterfalls spewed down the rocky slopes while the saturated air was clammy and cool. The two primary species preserved in this park are the Nilgiri tahr, a rare mountain goat, and the kurinji plant, which flowers once every twelve years, with bright blue blossoms.

Walking up the winding trail, I was reminded how many plants in these mountains are closely related to Himalayan species, though they are separated by a gap of 2,500 kilometres. At the side of the path, I recognized yellow raspberry bushes (*Rubus ellipticus*) that grow near my home in Landour. Even the fabled kurinji (*Strobilanthes kunthiana*) has a Himalayan relative, *Strobilanthes urticifolia*, which blooms every monsoon with tubular blue petals. Though the kurinji plants in Eravikulam would only flower again in 2030, the leaves and woody stems were recognizably similar. Plant poachers in the Western Ghats dig up this rare flora for medicinal purposes as well as for illegal sale to gardeners. One of the signs in the park expressed frustration: 'Neelakurinji, as it is locally known, are being plundered from the grasslands of the High Ranges by ignorant/berserk people.'

Like the kurinji, the Nilgiri tahr is endemic to the southern ranges of the Western and

Eastern Ghats, in Tamil Nadu and Kerala. Once hunted by tea planters, they are now strictly protected and listed as endangered on the IUCN Red List. An isolated population, these wild goats are related to Himalayan tahr, found in the upper reaches of Uttarakhand and Nepal. Unlike their Himalayan cousins, which are larger and have shaggy, reddish-brown coats, the Nilgiri tahr have short hair and are a pale grey colour, with a delicate black line down their spines.

While climbing to the upper boundary of the park's tourist zone, I was surprised to see two tahr grazing in a patch of grasses and ferns. They seemed untroubled by my presence and allowed me to approach within a few metres. Both were equipped with short, stout horns, and like all Caprinae, they had beautiful, attentive eyes. The tahrs' ghostly grey pelage seemed perfectly suited to the colourless mist that swept in around us. As I watched them move up the slope, the wild goats seemed to vanish like apparitions amidst the dense clouds.

## 3

## THE RAINS IN GOA

Traditionally, the monsoon has always been a time when travellers returned home after completing their journeys. The seas grew too rough for safe passage and roads were mired in mud. Rivers swelled with the rain and became impassable. Bridges and embankments washed away while ferries could not contend with the swift currents. Towns and villages were marooned like islands amidst the floodwaters that covered fields and lowlands. In the mountains, landslides blocked treacherous routes across ridges.

Along the coast, fishermen beached their vessels to spend time with their families, mending nets and exchanging stories. Traders returned from abroad and adjourned to their factories or counting houses to tally up the year's earnings. Caravans dispersed after unloading their cargo. Camels, bullocks, and horses were stabled, growing fat on green fodder and enjoying a respite as the rain poured down. Shepherds had no need to roam with their flocks in search of new pastures. Hunters unstrung their bows and set aside their spears. Game trails through the jungle were overgrown with creepers and nettles, the wet grass infested with leeches and venomous snakes. Itinerant minstrels and raconteurs paused their wanderings. Pilgrims returned from pious ramblings to regale their neighbours with tales of sacred sites and miraculous shrines. Mendicants retired to their caves. Soldiers remained in their barracks while muskets and cannons rusted, and gunpowder mouldered in damp magazines.

Though my instincts urged me to travel in pursuit of the monsoon, as Alexander Frater had done, I quickly realized that it might be wiser to stay at home and let the monsoon come to me. After my visit to Kerala, I retreated to Goa where my wife, Ameeta, and I have owned a small flat for the past twelve years. While Mussoorie remains my primary home, Goa provides us with a welcome escape from cold Himalayan winters. In that sense, I suppose we are climate migrants, enjoying the warmer temperatures and tropical greenery of Siolim, a small town where we now live for part of the year.

Arriving from Kerala, I found that it had been raining in Goa for almost a week and there was no doubt that the monsoon was here. While this season brings torrential storms it also fosters a quieter pace of life in Goa compared to the busy tourist season in December and January. The greenery becomes even more intense and sitting on the balcony of our flat, I looked out over a lush garden of flowering shrubs that attracts well over a hundred species of birds, from kingfishers and pittas to bulbuls and sunbirds. In the sky, white egrets were stencilled upon dark indigo clouds.

Every morning and evening, as if following a strict flight schedule, a flock of great hornbills winged their way over the treetops. When it rained, the areca nut palms swayed in the wind and shed the deluge like giant parasols, while the humid air felt almost cold.

One of the pleasures that precedes the monsoon in Goa and continues after the rains commence, are mangoes, which ripen at this time of year. As Vivek Menezes, an authority on all things Goan, explains

> Right from the eighteenth century, travellers and writers have agreed that there's no match for Goa's mangoes… the Fernandin and Xavier and Monserrate, and most especially, the indescribably sublime Hilario and Mankurad... The whole of Goa, from the Ghats to the Arabian Sea, comprises a mere sliver of the vast Subcontinent, but has developed more than 100 varieties of mangoes ever since the

> Jesuits introduced modern grafting techniques in the 16th century. Within just a couple of decades of that influx of European ideas, the results of the experiments had become acclaimed, treasured and celebrated wherever they reached across the known world.

Siolim is famous for its Hilario mangoes, commonly known as Manga Hilario or Mangilar. These originated from a single tree grafted by Hilario Fernandez, a wealthy nineteenth century landowner in the town. One morning, soon after returning to Siolim, I went in search of the mother tree. Eventually, I found it growing next to an elegant blue and white bungalow dating back to 1852. The property is now run as a guest house called Hilario's and the manager, Munawar, guided me through the house to the backyard where the enormous tree, at least 20 metres tall, loomed over a swimming pool. Unfortunately, I was too late to taste the mangoes, most of which Munawar told me had been eaten by langur monkeys and birds. However, at the fruit market in Mapusa, near our home, I found plenty of Alphonso mangoes, which are celebrated as one of the finest varieties in India. With firm, buttery flesh of a saffron hue, they are named after Afonso de Albuquerque, the Portuguese admiral who conquered Goa in 1510.

Though we avoid Goa's beaches in winter because of the crowds, during the monsoon they are almost empty of tourists. A few days after I returned from Kochi, Ameeta and I went to Morjim, our closest beach, for an evening walk. Other than a makeshift stall selling coconuts, no other vendors were in sight and the shacks that usually line the shore had been dismantled. The sea was rough, with waves more than 2 metres high, the water steel grey in the overcast light. At the northern end of the beach, a few reckless tourists waded into the surf while lifeguards patrolled the sand and stray dogs chased each other in circles. A gusty wind was blowing off the water. Unlike in Kochi, the sky was a mass of billowing clouds. Beyond the headland south of us, where the ruins of Chapora Fort overlooks the sea, curtains of blue rain were falling offshore. But on Morjim Beach nothing more than a fine drizzle sifted through the air, as light as sea spray. Though the setting sun remained hidden, the evening light began to change, a peculiar jaundiced colour that filtered through the clouds and cast a metallic sheen on the waves, as if they had turned from steel to copper and bronze.

Several men with hand-held throw nets were casting into the surf but the fleet of fishing vessels that we usually see along Morjim were all drawn back in amongst the coconut trees, 50 metres from the shore. In an effort to protect endangered species of marine life, Goa enforces a fishing ban on boats and trawlers during the monsoon. It is also a safety precaution, for the sea can be dangerous at this time of year and many lives have been lost in the past. Vivek Menezes tells me that because of the fishing ban many Goans resort to eating dried fish and prawns at this time of year, as well as freshwater species from ponds and rivers. There are also a number of wild delicacies to be foraged and eaten during the monsoon. Olmi mushrooms, which grow on termite castles, are a favourite addition to Goan cuisine during the rains. Though now illegal, Menezes explains that villagers traditionally collected paddy snails and 'jumping chickens', a euphemism for bullfrog's legs.

Soon after the onset of the monsoon, the town of Siolim celebrates the annual Festival of Sao João on 24 June. This is the Feast of St. John the Baptist that commemorates a New Testament account of Mary's visit to her cousin Elizabeth in Judea. The two women, both of whom were pregnant, greeted each other and we are told that Elizabeth was possessed by the Holy Spirit as 'the babe leaped for joy in her womb'. Mary stayed with Elizabeth for three months until John was born and then returned to her husband, Joseph, after which she gave birth to Jesus, another three months later. In the Gregorian calendar, these two events correspond to the summer and winter solstice. For the Catholic community in Goa, the Sao João Festival recalls an important biblical event, but it is also a celebration of the coming of the rains. A small chapel dedicated to John the Baptist is situated in Siolim, where newly married couples make offerings of fruit and flowers to ensure they conceive a child. One of the traditions of the Sao João Festival is that young men jump into their neighbours' wells to commemorate the baby leaping in its mother's womb.

St. Anthony's Church lies at the heart of Siolim, facing a narrow estuary connecting Chapora Bay to a freshwater wetland that extends for several kilometres to the east of the town. During the festival, a parade of boats sails in from the sea along the tidal waterway to the church. Freshly painted in bright colours, with elaborate decorations, the boats compete for prizes while popular bands play on a stage nearby. A lively, carefree spirit accompanies this flotilla, though one of the boats this year had a theme of illegal construction, depicting a traditional Goan home overshadowed by a looming high-rise building. Another boat carried a replica of a village well. From mid-afternoon until long after dark, both residents and tourists gathered in the centre of Siolim. Most of them wore floral crowns, called 'kopel', made of fresh blossoms and creepers, which evoke the light-hearted spirit of a midsummer night's dream. And when monsoon showers burst from the clouds it only added to the excitement and revelry.

Thirty-five years ago, this festival was revived by a group of Siolim residents, led by Alex Fernandes, a well-known artist who signs his work 'Alexyz'. In the 1970s, he moved back to Goa from Bombay, where he was working as a political cartoonist and illustrator. Mario Miranda, Goa's best-known cartoonist, was a mentor and friend. Alexyz's satirical drawings cast a sharp eye on contentious issues like the agitation for Goa's statehood and protests in support of the Konkani language. He and other activists of his generation were keen to preserve and promote Goan culture, traditions, and the natural environment. One of his cartoons is of a jovial man wearing a floral crown and jumping into a well during the Sao João Festival, while his wife shouts a warning: 'Forsu, don't jump in the well! Some hotel has dumped all its garbage in it!'

'We started the boat festival in Siolim on a very small scale,' Alexyz recalled when we met, 'raising funds from local residents...a hundred rupees here, fifty there. Prizes were given for the most creatively decorated boats and for the best floral crowns. Now it's become a huge thing and the politicians have got involved. The organizers spend lakhs of rupees.' He stopped himself and then shrugged. 'But I suppose people still enjoy themselves....'

At the age of eighty, Alexyz continues to

live in Siolim with his wife, Tecla. A spry, slender man with a trimmed, grey beard and a shy yet generous smile, he spoke softly but with a firm sense of commitment to the causes he has supported throughout his life.

'Many of my cartoons were used on protest posters,' he told me. 'People waited for them in the newspaper every morning. My editor sometimes gave me eight columns a day!'

When I complained that there are hardly any political cartoons in the press these days, Alexyz nodded. 'People are too cautious now and the newspapers are all owned by business houses who don't want to offend politicians.'

Seated in his drawing room, with an assortment of framed caricatures on the wall behind him, Alexyz reminisced about the idealism and strong sense of Goan identity that brought him back from Bombay to Siolim. He also expressed regrets over the many ways in which Goa has changed and developed since then.

'Our main street used to be a mud road

and now look,' he said. 'It's been widened and so many trees were cut down, not for us but for the tourist traffic.'

Even the monsoon is no longer what it used to be.

'Earlier, during the rains, we used to hear frogs every night, like an orchestra outside,' he told me. 'But the town is now so built up, the frogs have gone silent.'

On a lighter note, another of Alexyz's cartoons has the chief of the weather bureau standing on his desk in a flooded office with an umbrella over his head, looking harassed and speaking to someone on the phone. He announces that he's going to take early retirement because he can't predict the monsoon.

As we spoke, there was a downpour outside, rainwater sluicing off the eaves of the house and cascading into the yard below.

After a while our conversation circled back to the Sao João Festival. Local musicians, including Remo Fernandes, the famous pop star and songwriter, whose hometown is Siolim, have performed at the festival. One of Remo's recent recordings, released in 2024, is entitled, 'Rain, Rain, Rain'. The accompanying video was shot in Goa during the monsoon and includes images of rain falling on lush paddy fields, mango trees, and the back streets of Siolim, while the nostalgic lyrics evoke the constant showers of this season:

*Rain, Rain, Rain*
*You wash away my pain, pain, pain...*
*You keep whispering her name, name,*
*name*
*Oh, lovely monsoon rain,*
*Oh, lovely Goa rain.*

'Siolim has always been known for its musicians,' Alexyz explained. 'There's a long musical tradition here with people like Antoninho "Anthony" de Souza, who used to perform on the radio when the Portuguese still ruled Goa. But the most famous of all was Joãzinho "Johnson" Carvalho who had a dance band called "Johnson and His Jolly

Boys". They were so popular that people would postpone their weddings just to make sure he could perform. This was in the days before there were amplifiers and Johnson would sing with a megaphone. Mario has drawn wonderful cartoons of him and his band.'

As the gentle drumming of rain on palm trees outside set a calming tempo in the late afternoon, I took my leave. Alexyz walked me out, past the traditional well in his yard, which is a fixture of old Goan homes. On his front gate is a sign: 'Beware of God'. Despite all of the unwelcome changes that have occurred in Siolim, the light drizzle that dimpled pools of water on the ground evoked the timeless constancy of the monsoon.

# 4

# ORIGINS OF THE MONSOON

According to Vedic mythology, the advent of the monsoon can be traced back to a titanic conflict between Indra, 'lord of the firmament', and Vritrasura, a powerful demon who was responsible for drought and held the earth's waters captive, including South Asia's ancient rivers. Indra rode into battle on his war elephant, Airavata, who had six tusks and three trunks and was as white as a cumulus cloud. Vritrasura, often depicted as a giant serpent, 'is described as having neither feet nor hands, and Vedic hymns speak of his frightening hissing and snorting. He caused thunder, lightning, mist and hail, and was constantly at war with Indra...who frequently overpowered him with his thunderbolts and thus compelled him to release the rain'. Eventually, after a prolonged struggle in which both combatants were assisted by other deities and demons, Indra finally destroyed Vritrasura, using a thunderbolt, 'Vajrayudha', made from the bones of a saintly rishi, Dadhichi. This celestial battle, described in both the Vedas and the Puranas, with some variation and considerable embellishment, evokes the violent genesis of the monsoon, as thunder and lightning echo the clashing forces of good and evil.

Meanwhile, science presents us with a very different account of thc monsoon's genesis, though the story is equally dramatic and also plays out on an epic scale. Roughly 160 million years ago, when the primal continent Pangea began to split apart, the landmass that would eventually become the Indian subcontinent was still attached to Africa. Beginning around 88 million years ago, during a prolonged series of volcanic eruptions, India broke away from the eastern coast of Madagascar and began to move northwards, propelled by the tectonic forces of continental drift. In this process, the Indian Ocean formed in the wake of the subcontinent, as it was driven further and further away from its original position on earth. Eventually, when India came in contact with Asia, somewhere between 60 to 25 million years ago, depending on which geologist tells the tale, the force of this collision fractured the earth's crust and pushed layers of rock thousands of metres into the sky, forming the Himalaya and Tibetan Plateau.

Significant meteorological changes accompanied this geological event, as the mountains rose to higher elevations where temperatures were colder and snow collected on the summits. Over time, as the earth experienced a series of ice ages, spreading glaciers extended across most of the Himalaya. Meanwhile, the Tibetan Plateau remained relatively dry and was never covered by an ice cap. As these arid plains warmed during summer, the resulting air currents began to draw evaporating moisture from equatorial oceans far away to the south. This seasonal cycle eventually became what we call the southwest monsoon. As in all creation myths, these events occurred long before human beings walked the earth. Even as scientists attempt to piece together a probable chain of cause and effect, there will always remain inexplicable elements of mystery to these climatic phenomena.

Astrologers inform us that the arrival of the monsoon coincides with the sun's passage through the Mrigashira (deer's head) constellation, one of twenty-seven 'lunar mansions' or nakshatras. In 2025, Mrigasira Karte, a festival that celebrates this celestial event, fell on 8 June, or the twelfth day of the Hindu month of Jyestha. The monsoon continues through the months of Ashadha and Shravan (Sawan), finally ending at the beginning of Bhadra, roughly in mid-September. A series of festivals and pilgrimages coincide with the rainy season. In North India, the Kavar Yatra occurs during Shravan, when hundreds of thousands of devotees travel by foot, carrying holy water from the Ganga in Haridwar to their villages and homes. There is also the festival of Teej, which is celebrated with swings that recreate monsoon breezes. And Naga Panchami, when cobras are worshipped. Towards the end of the monsoon, the Ganesh Chaturthi festival is celebrated in which images of Ganapati are enshrined in homes and public spaces before the idols are finally immersed in the sea or in lakes and ponds. Each of these religious events are tied to the climate and venerate water as an essential element of life.

Attempting to predict the unpredictable, meteorologists examine many different indicators to forecast the monsoon—not just the date and time of its arrival but also its progress northwards as well as the intensity and duration of the resulting rainfall. In the end, however, too many competing factors and elements of uncertainty exist for anyone to calculate precisely what will occur, even if we know exactly what generates the winds and clouds that storm across South Asia from late June to early September.

As any textbook will tell you, the monsoon is caused by energy from the sun heating the waters of the Indian Ocean near the Equator. Evaporation from the sea rises into the atmosphere to form clouds. Meanwhile, our planet continues to rotate on its axis, though the airborne moisture no longer moves in concert with the surface of the earth below. At the same time, through a process of convection, heated air rises skyward creating thermal currents at different levels in the atmosphere. The force of the wind changes constantly, as does its path, according to a range of factors that are often connected to distant events beyond the horizon, even as far away as the North Atlantic or the South Pacific.

In 1963, a meteorologist at MIT, Edward Lorenz published a scientific paper with the uninspiring title, 'Deterministic Nonperiodic Flow'. In this paper he argued that a minor, seemingly random event in one part of the world can have serious climatic consequences somewhere else, even thousands of kilometres away. This radical idea was popularized in a simple analogy referred to as the 'Butterfly Effect'. In essence, Lorenz suggested that if a butterfly in the Amazon rainforests fluttered its wings the resulting change in air pressure could ultimately generate a tornado in North America. This seemingly absurd correlation between minuscule changes in the atmosphere and catastrophic meteorological events had its own revolutionary effect on modern scientific and mathematical thought. The Butterfly Effect became the foundation of Chaos Theory, which is now applied to everything from economics to evolution.

If we adapt Lorenz's analogy to the monsoon, we could say that when a lone yak, grazing on the Tibetan Plateau, whisks its tail to brush off a fly, the resulting turbulence in the air can set off a chain reaction that results in millions of tonnes of seawater from the Indian Ocean ascending into the sky from where it is borne by fierce winds from equatorial latitudes to the highest mountains on earth. Whether or not this occurs in that particular sequence, meteorologists have long known that there is a direct correlation between the warming of the Tibetan Plateau, which produces the fresh grass on which our unsuspecting yak feeds, and the southwest monsoon. These seasonal changes in temperature generate sustained air currents that draw condensed moisture from the warming waters between Africa and India towards the subcontinent until ultimately the Himalaya receive a considerable share of the resulting precipitation.

Meteorologists have studied the extended history of the monsoon, over millions of years, to better understand weather patterns that might occur in the future, particularly in the context of our current concern over climate change. In this process, they have discovered another beguiling variation on the Butterfly Effect in the coastal waters of the Arabian Sea. In 1991, scientists examining core samples of sediment from the seabed off the shoreline of Oman were able to assert that the 'abundance' of a species of plankton, *Globigerina bulloides*, in any one year, was a key indicator of 'the summer monsoon wind strength'. These minute marine organisms are widely distributed and flourish under certain conditions depending on the temperature of the water and the nutrients it contains. Palaeobotanists working alongside climatologists have established a clear link between *G. bulloides* plankton blooms and favourable monsoon conditions over hundreds of millennia.

Equally compelling is the fact that many of the nutrients on which these minuscule life forms depend are carried by winds from the southern Sahara that deposit tonnes of blowing sand and dust into the Arabian Sea. The airborne particles settle and dissolve in the seawater fertilizing the plankton, which flourish and then die off, ultimately becoming part of the sediment that settles to the ocean floor. Core samples extracted from the seabed off the coast of Oman contain evidence of prehistoric sandstorms that swept eastwards across the Red Sea and the Arabian Peninsula. These sediments preserve and mark a climatic timeline reaching back to the Cenozoic Era, somewhere around 35 million years ago, when the subcontinent of India collided with Asia and the Tibetan Plateau was pushed upward along with the Himalaya.

The monsoon consists not only of air currents and clouds but also dust particles from the deserts of North Africa that are carried from arid, seemingly sterile landscapes to the tropical forests of India. These nutrients, along with the moisture swept inland by monsoon winds contribute to the fecund diversity of life on the subcontinent. This demonstrates how climatic events like the monsoon are not isolated in time or space but are dynamic, ever-changing phenomena linked to everything from continental drift, butterfly wings or yak tails, dust plumes, as well as the brief life cycle of plankton.

The Roman historian, Pliny the Elder, credited a Greek sailor and trader named Hippalus with the 'discovery' of the monsoon, sometime during the first century CE. Undoubtedly, voyagers from Arabia and India already knew of these strong gales and used them to cross the oceans. Roman, Egyptian, Phoenician, and other traders from around the Mediterranean used the 'Hippalus winds', as Pliny dubbed them, to navigate a route from the Red Sea to India, which provided a quicker and less hazardous alternative to overland journeys. Gold and silver coins that were used to purchase spices, perfumes, ivory, and other exotic merchandise have been found along the Malabar and Coromandel coasts, while live tigers and elephants were shipped from India for the colosseum in Rome.

The name, 'monsoon', is a corruption of the Arabic word, 'mausim', which means season. It was used by Indian and Arab pilots, who assisted Vasco da Gama and other Portuguese captains to sail from Madagascar and the Maldives to

Indian ports like Calicut, Cochin, and Goa. Experienced mariners used the stars to calculate the onset of seasonal gales that swept eastwards, as well as gentler westerly winds that followed the monsoon, carrying ships in the opposite direction. These annual trade winds provided a reasonably reliable passage to and from India, though as Vasco da Gama discovered on one of his return journeys, they could dissipate unpredictably and leave a fleet becalmed for weeks on end.

Portuguese merchants and writers transliterated mausim as monção or moução. Dutch traders who followed them to the East, further altered the spelling to monssoyn and monssoen from which the name, as we now spell it, navigated its way into English usage. Along with the traders, these seasonal winds brought with them new faiths. The apostle Thomas, who came as a missionary to India during the first years of the Christian Era, would have sailed from the Holy Land through the Red Sea and been carried by monsoon winds to the Kerala coast, where he established the Marthoma Church whose congregants are the earliest followers of Jesus in India. Jewish traders from the Middle East and North Africa also brought their beliefs and traditions with them and established synagogues in port cities like Cochin. The advent of Islam dates back to the seventh century CE. Soon after the Prophet Muhammad received the divine wisdom of the Quran, these teachings were carried to the western coast of India by Arab sailors, well before Islam arrived by overland routes.

For something as ethereal and elusive as air currents and water vapour stirring above the surface of uncharted oceans between the Cape of Good Hope and the Isle of Serendib, the southwest monsoon has had enormous geographical, biological, cultural, economic, political, and social consequences, not just for India and Asia but for the rest of the world. In primordial times, after the mass extinctions of the Cretaceous era, 66 million years ago, when 75 per cent of all life forms were lost, the climatic conditions that accompanied India's subcontinental migration and the orogenesis of the Himalaya, helped a vast number of new species to evolve. All of the great rivers of the subcontinent, which the serpent demon Vritrasura held captive in his coils, depend on the monsoon.

The arrival of *Homo sapiens* in South Asia and our eventual shift from hunting–gathering to settled, agrarian societies like the Indus Valley Civilization was driven by the critical cycle of annual rains. It is not an exaggeration to say that every culture that has existed in India was nurtured and shaped by the presence of the monsoon, while in more recent times it brought colonial conquest from Europe to these shores. Some historians would also argue that the rise of the freedom movement and the fall of British imperialism was a direct consequence of several failed monsoons and horrific droughts that caused famines during the early part of the twentieth century.

# 5

# INTO THE JUNGLE

In the darkness, our torch beams pick up the first stray drops of rain filtering through a layered canopy of foliage overhead. For a few seconds, the surrounding forest becomes agitated, a restless murmuring of wet leaves. Then, all at once, before I can put away my camera and open an umbrella, a sudden downpour descends upon us. Already wet from two earlier cloudbursts that caught me unawares, the only part of my body that is still dry are my feet inside a pair of rubber gumboots, though I can now feel a trickle of water running down my right ankle.

Walking through a jungle in Goa during the monsoon is a totally immersive experience. Even when it's not raining, the humidity is close to 100 per cent. Tonight, we are searching for reptiles, amphibians, insects, arachnids, and any other creatures that emerge after dark—an activity popularly known as 'herping'. Omkar Dharwadkar, with whom I've taken similar excursions in the past, is leading the way, along with his colleague, Kuldip Topo. One of Goa's most experienced naturalists, Omkar is co-founder of Mrugaya Xpeditions, an ecotourism company that specializes in birding and wildlife.

After a few minutes, the rain subsides and we continue our quest, shining torches into the underbrush and along the margins of an unpaved forest road that marks the periphery of Bhagwan Mahavir Wildlife Sanctuary. On the leafy stems of a waist-high shrub, Omkar points out two atlas moth caterpillars. A chalky white colour with a greenish tinge, they are each about the size of my thumb. Voraciously feeding on leaves, the caterpillars look like fat wads of cotton wool. Nothing in their appearance suggests that they will eventually be transformed into one of the largest moths on earth, with a 20–25 centimetre wingspan and elaborate coppery brown patterns. The wingtips on an atlas moth resemble the head of a snake, which deters predators. Omkar explains that the adult moths have no mouths and live for only a few days, during which time they breed and then starve to death.

Ten steps further on, submerged in a large puddle of water, is a skittering frog, its body the same murky tan as the mud. Already this evening, we have seen six different species of amphibians, five frogs, and one common toad. At the beginning of our walk, before dusk, we traversed a laterite plateau. The hard red rock was full of crevices and cavities in which rainwater collects. Hiding in these tiny pockets of moisture were Goa cricket frogs, no more than a couple centimetres long. The same colour as wet laterite, their high-pitched calls sound like chirping insects. Also on the plateau, in a stunted terminalia tree, overhanging a larger pond, Kuldip spotted a female Malabar gliding frog perfectly camouflaged in the leaves. Lime green, she was about 10 centimetres long. The remnants of her foam nest clung to a nearby branch, though it was now empty as the tadpoles had already hatched and dropped into the water below. Re-entering the forest, Omkar identified a reddish burrowing frog half-hidden amidst the leaf litter. And, as twilight faded into shadows, tiny Amboli bush frogs and their Bombay cousins set up a cacophony of loud croaks and clicks. Their calls are amplified by balloon-like vocal sacks that inflate below their throats. No creatures are more at home in the monsoon than frogs, which multiply with the rain, as if falling from the clouds.

An abundance of amphibians inevitably attracts plenty of snakes, which feast on the frogs and toads that proliferate at this time of year. In a single evening, at different points along our path, we come upon four hump-nosed pit vipers. The first of these is a juvenile, hardly 20 centimetres long, though it is poised within the leaf litter, like a coiled watch spring, waiting to ambush whatever prey comes near.

The other three vipers are all adults, over twice as long, with thicker bodies. Their venom isn't fatal for human beings but can cause serious complications, including renal failure. No anti-venom is currently available to treat a hump-nosed pit viper's bite. A pale fawn colour with black dots and dashes on its lower body, it has an easily recognizable triangular head, though the hump on its nose is only visible upon closer examination. Omkar tells me that these are the most common venomous species in this forest, though there are also cobras, kraits, and saw-scaled vipers, as well as a variety of non-venomous snakes including pythons. Malabar pit vipers are found several hundred metres higher in the Western Ghats.

Just before nightfall, a shadowy herd of gaur cross our path and disappear into the cover of tangled tree limbs and creepers. These huge wild cattle are the largest animals in Goa's forests, which have no elephant herds. Though occasionally the gaur can charge human beings on foot, if threatened, they prefer to move away and leave us alone. The other mammal we encounter on our night walk is an Indian giant squirrel. Silhouetted high above us in the trees, it ignores our presence for several minutes before darting off as another deluge of rain begins to fall.

Once the downpour has ended, I follow Omkar and Kuldip off the forest road and along an overgrown trail between dripping curtains of leaves. After 20 metres or so, we stop to examine an array of bracket mushrooms on a fallen tree trunk. They remind me of coral formations under the sea, with flared shapes and variegated hues of rust and umber. A few steps further on, we switch off our torches and the darkness is complete. The bush frogs continue gossiping nearby and I can hear a repeated hooting whistle that sounds like an owl. Omkar identifies it as a slaty-legged crake, a shy forest bird similar in size and shape to a moorhen.

As my eyes adjust to the darkness, I begin to see a pale glow in front of us, as if a diffused beam of moonlight were shining on the trunk and roots of a tree. A bluish-green aura, this eerie light comes from one of several species of bioluminescent fungi found in Goa's forests during the monsoon. Glancing around, I can see a few other patches of illumination. Invisible during the day, these microscopic fungi appear only as a gauzy sheen in the darkness. As if beamed in from distant galaxies, their faint lustre seems to shine like an ethereal enigma. At the same time, a couple of glow-worms display bright beads of phosphorescence in the leaf litter at our feet while overhead, amidst the branches, fireflies switch their lanterns on and off as they flit through the darkness. Entomologists have discovered that each species of firefly gives off its own pattern of blinking lights, like coded semaphore, to attract a suitable mate.

Eventually, a swollen stream blocks our path, and we decide to turn back. Scanning a ruined wall of laterite bricks nearby, covered in ferns and moss, my torch picks up no signs of life but when Omkar switches on an ultraviolet light, we can see a dozen or more scorpions glowing in the dark. Their segmented bodies and sharp pincers reflect the UV beam with a neon brightness that looks radioactive. Retracing our route along the forest road, we encounter a variety of nocturnal insects such as an Indian owlet moth, which is drying its wings. Two large spots on either side look like a bird's round eyes and its abdomen resembles a curved beak. Omkar also spots a tiger beetle resting on a leaf. No bigger than a grain of rice it is an iridescent blue and green, like a polished gem.

By the time we get back to our vehicles, most of the frogs have fallen silent and only a few night sounds persist—the whistling call of a frogmouth and the sharp cry of a slender loris—though we are unable to spot either creature. Another burst of rain descends upon us, and I duck into my car, after saying a hurried goodbye to Omkar, who is returning home. Frantically pulling on his raingear, Kuldip starts his scooter and leads me along a maze of forest roads and detours, to the village of Talde, where I am spending the night. The scooter's red tail light is barely visible in the rain but soon after we pass through the main gate of Mahavir Bhagwan Wildlife Sanctuary, Kuldip makes an abrupt U-turn. Realizing that he must have seen a snake crossing the road, I stop my car, though I can't see anything in front of me as the pounding rain disperses the twin beams from my headlights. The paved road is a fast-flowing river, 10 centimetres deep. Parking his scooter, Kuldip, rushes toward me and when I roll down the driver-side window, I see a pale, slithering shape disappearing under my vehicle.

Grabbing its tail, Kuldip draws it back out onto the road and picks it up, the slippery creature writhing in his hands. Over half a metre long and a silvery grey colour, it looks more like an eel or giant earthworm than a snake. Known as caecilians, these limbless amphibians are seldom seen and when they are found they've often been run over by cars. Squirming out of Kuldip's hands, the caecilian glides away through the flowing rainwater and disappears into the dead leaves and weeds at the side of the road. Washing his hands and wiping them on ferns, Kuldip rinses off the slimy mucous-like substance that the caecilian secretes in self-defence.

Five minutes later, when we reach our homestay in Talde village, Kuldip tells me that it was a Bombay caecilian (*Ichthyophis peninsularis*), one of more than thirty species found in the Western Ghats. Though non-venomous, its secretions can irritate your eyes if you touch your face without properly washing your hands. Very little is known about caecilians and only recently have scientists studied their morphology, distribution, and behaviour, for they live in the soil and only emerge during the monsoon.

Later, after we've eaten dinner, prepared by village women who run the homestay, Kuldip tells me that he wants to show me 'another magical thing'. By now the rain has ceased and we put on our gumboots again to walk a hundred metres beyond the neighbouring homes. Near an ancient temple complex, dating back to the fourteenth century, lies a sacred grove. The entwined branches overhead are still dripping as we pass beneath them. Stopping beside the broad bole of a tree, we turn off our torches. After a minute or two, small bluish spots of light appear on the smooth bark, another variety of bioluminescent fungi. Unlike the earlier species we saw, which was microscopic, this consists of tiny mushrooms that measure half a centimetre across. Their delicate gills are like the furled petals of a budding flower. Despite the clammy warmth of the night, they look like drops of rain that have frozen into pale beads of ice, speckling the tree trunk.

During the rest of the night, it continues to rain heavily, though I am dry inside the mud walls and tiled roof of the homestay. Early the next morning, when we emerge onto the veranda to a cloudy dawn, an assortment of birds arrive and depart from a spreading mango tree in the yard outside, its branches draped with orchids. Red-whiskered bulbuls squabble with each other while a pair of common iora add flashes of yellow amidst the dark foliage. A grey hornbill flies past with syncopated wing beats. Further off, I hear a black-hooded oriole calling and finally spot its gold plumage in a jackfruit tree. A white-throated kingfisher is perched on a single electric line and at the top of a dead tree, a lone shikra surveys the ground for lizards and skinks.

Talde village is surrounded by thick jungle and lies at the foot of the Western Ghats. Forested ridges rise above us in the shifting mist. A scattered settlement of about two dozen homes, this remote hamlet marks the end of the road. A little later in the morning, Kuldip takes me for a walk along a jungle trail that leads into a valley beyond the village.

Though the rain has stopped, our clothes are soon soaked as we brush our way through the overgrown plants and shrubs that lean across the trail. Giant wood spiders with yellow-striped bodies and a legspan as big as my palm have constructed webs across our path. Droplets of water cling to the woven filaments. On a bush nearby, Kuldip turns over a leaf to reveal a tiny snail with symmetrical bands of brown and white on its spiral shell.

I can hear the river to our left long before I see it, a swift torrent overflowing its banks. Last night's rain in the hills above Talde has flooded the stream, which washes through the jungle, flattening shrubs and saplings. One of the trees that Kuldip points out looks like a guava, with small green fruit, though he tells me it is actually a 'false guava' (*Catunaregam spinosa*). On closer inspection, I can see the branches have thorns. Villagers dry and crush the fruit, which is used to stun fish in rivers and ponds.

Kuldip also picks up a seed about the size

of a hen's egg. Flattened and with a dark brown hull, it comes from one of the woody creepers (*Entada rheedii*) that have wrapped themselves around some of the forest trees. Kuldip explains that though the seeds are mildly poisonous, tribal communities in Goa collect them and soak them in a flowing stream, so the water washes away the toxins, after which they crush them into a coarse flour that is mixed with jaggery to make laddoos. Another common shrub that Kuldip identifies is *Mussaenda frundosa*, also called the white flag or dhobi tree. Though most of the leaves are green, it sprouts a random number of white leaves that look like bleached handkerchiefs tied to the branches. This foliage is often used in religious ceremonies, as decoration, particularly during the Ganesh Chaturthi festival.

Kuldip's hometown is Usgao, about 30 kilometres southwest of Talde. He grew up in these forests and has first-hand knowledge of the flora, their medicinal uses and which plants are toxic, and which are edible. After completing an

MA in Zoology from Goa University, Kuldip spent a couple of years working for the Mineral Foundation of Goa, as part of a team engaged in community based ecotourism. Last year he joined Mrugya Xpeditions as a naturalist and guide. He has always had an interest in the outdoors, especially birdwatching. Though the monsoon is not the best time of year to see Goa's avifauna, we come across an interesting range of species including an orange-headed thrush, a white-rumped shama, and a dark-fronted babbler, each of them skulking in the undergrowth. We also see several flocks of Malabar parakeets raiding the mango trees.

Returning to the village, we visit the old temple at Talde, which is dedicated to the goddess Brahmini Mata. Most of the shrine is a relatively recent construction with concrete walls and terracotta tiles on the roof but the plinth is much older. As we circle around it, a light drizzle begins to fall. The carved stones along the temple's foundation depict images of Hanuman, with simian features and a long tail, as well as stylized tigers that look more like folk art than classical temple sculptures. Several images of cobras are carved in the stone, most prominently on the front steps of the shrine. There is also a bas-relief of the goddess holding two cobras. Another chiselled image depicts a pair of copulating figures, though their erotic love play is discretely shielded by a fern that grows out of a crack in the rocks. A large, rectangular frieze shows a line of dancing figures and drummers, a common motif in tribal art. Kuldip tells me that every year during March, a celebration is held at this temple, known as Fulansho Khel, a spring flower festival. The men in the village enter the forest to the accompaniment of ghoomat drums and make offerings to a large stone or Deva Pathar deep in the jungle.

Clearly, this shrine, which dates back to the fourteenth century, is dedicated to deities rooted in nature. Tigers and peacocks proliferate on the plinth, chiselled out of red basalt, which has weathered and turned almost black. The sacred grove surrounding the temple, where we saw glowing fungi last night, is littered with stone carvings scattered amidst the trees and plants. Three of these are Gajalakshmi images, which often adorn the gateway of a temple. Lying in the open and covered with moss, the goddess is seated between two elephants with their trunks raised. The verdure of the moss gives the carvings a velvety texture, as if the monsoon has brought the stones to life.

# 6

# THE MONSOON AS METAPHOR

In poetry, art, and music, the monsoon evokes a complex range of moods and emotions, many of which are associated with longing and desire. The anticipation of rain after the dry heat of summer suggests an erotic tension, reflected in the gathering clouds, accompanied by thunder and lightning. When the first drops fall, unrequited passions are finally released with the consummation of the monsoon.

The *Gathasaptasati* is among the first anthologies of classical Indian verse. Attributed to the Satavahana king Hala, it was compiled in the second century CE and contains 700 poems in Prakrit, most of which celebrate sexual pleasure. Many of these short poems, translated into English by Arvind Krishna Mehrotra, probably predated the *Gathasaptasati* itself by several centuries and represent some of the earliest and most intimate poetic imagery linked to the monsoon.

> Thunderclouds in the sky,
>     Paths overgrown, streams in flood,
> And you, innocent one, in the window,
>     Expecting him.

As Mehrotra explains in the introduction to his anthology, *The Absent Traveller*, 'Metaphors take longer than a few centuries to fade if they fade at all, and Kalidasa and the classical Tamil poets...drew on Prakrit conventions and relocated them in their own literatures.' Sexual love play is sometimes overtly described in these poems but also suggested through subtle motifs and innuendo. Different species of monsoon flowers, from the inflorescence of kadamba trees to fragrant jasmine blossoms are used to indicate and arouse various aspects of sexual fulfilment. Infidelity and jealousy are interwoven with declarations of undying love and devotion. A sense of anxiety and doubt often accompanies a lover's absence, as in these verses by a female Tamil Sangam poet, Okkur Masathiyar.

> The rainy season
> has arrived, cool and fragrant.
> It laughs at me
> from the rain-fed bushes,
> showing its white teeth
> of jasmine buds.
> It seems to say:
> 'Her husband did not care
> for her wasting youth
> and went in search of riches.
> He isn't back home yet.
> Who knows where he is?'

The feminine voice seems best suited to invoking the monsoon, as in the words of Vidya, whose poem serves as an epigraph for this book. One of the first women to write Sanskrit love lyrics, sometime between the seventh and the ninth century of our current era, Vidya is known only by one name, though it is spelled in different ways, sometimes as Vijjaka or Vijja. Nothing else remains of her life story beyond the verses she composed. Translated by Andrew Schelling, her love songs, some erotic and others mournful, remind us of the enduring passions of the monsoon.

Kalidasa, who probably wrote his Sanskrit poems and plays in the fifth century CE, echoes the metaphors of classical Prakrit and Tamil poets. His verse narrative, *Meghaduta* (The Cloud Messenger) is a lyrical account of a monsoon cloud that conveys a message from a lovelorn yaksha (forest spirit), living in exile, who pines for his beloved. Another work by Kalidasa, *Ritusamhara*, is an anthology of shorter poems about different seasons of the year. The monsoon is depicted as a period of fertility and fruitfulness, as well as a time for reunion and lovemaking.

Their rocks caressed
by rain-filled clouds,

and flowing water
on all sides,
with a host of peacocks
ready to dance,
the hills now foster
moods of longing.

For Kalidasa, the natural world is full of lyrical images that underscore the romance of each season, especially the monsoon. He was a keen observer of flora and fauna, recognizing that the courtship rituals of peacocks signalled the advent of the rains. He also describes the Indragopa insects, or red velvet mites (*Trombidium grandissimum*) that appear with the onset of the monsoon. These are gathered and crushed to make a crimson dye. Kalidasa often refers to specific species of flowering plants like ketaki, the fragrant flower of the screw pine, which is distilled into a potent perfume. In some poems, the unpredictable monsoon weather personifies the traveller, whose delayed arrival suggests amorous digressions.

The wayward wind, wanderer in the
sky,
Cooled by the touch of the fresh clean
raindrops,
Rustles the leaves of trees
Bowed with the load of flowers,
And makes them dance;
Fragrant with the charming odour
Of the golden pollen of the ketaki,
It steals the hearts of lonely lovers.

The idea that seasonal rains accompany the return of a wandering lover whose indiscretions will be forgiven, at least briefly, in the throes of passion, is a recurring theme in Indian poetry, whatever its region or language. The fourteenth century Indo-Persian poet, Amir Khusrao, composed a ghazal that opened with the lines:

The cloud rains as I leave my beloved
What can a heart do parting from its
love on a day like this?'

One of the poetic conventions that evolved

over centuries after Kalidasa composed his *Ritusamhara*, was a cycle of poems that celebrated the seasons. Following in this tradition were the Barahmasa, or songs of twelve months, in which poets in Urdu and Hindi composed lyrical descriptions of the weather and all that came with it. The Sufi poet Da'ud, from Awadh, writes of the oppressive month in which the monsoon comes to an end:

> Now the heavy month of Bhadon has
> come, hard, unbearable:
> how will I fill these dark nights?
> Empty is my house, my husband is
> elsewhere,
> my couch is a snake, it bites again and
> again.
> I am alone, holding to a bed-prop,
> eyes wide open, heart burst till I die.
> Flashes of lightning, roar of thunder—
> they torment me:
> *viraha* like death itself has clutched my
> soul.

And the nineteenth century master of Urdu and Farsi poetry, Mirza Ghalib, evokes a subtle melancholy and deep sense of loneliness in this season.

> How does one pass the dark monsoon night?
> Alas, my eyes have become
> accustomed to counting the stars.

Commenting on this couplet, the literary scholar, Sunil Sharma writes: 'Even as the monsoon remained a metaphor for separation and sorrow by this time, the poet seemed to revel in his solitariness, but with all the despair it was the hope of seeing his beloved again that kept him on course.'

These ambivalent and conflicted emotions have been employed by poets for generations and continue today. In a poem entitled *Monsoon Journey*, Eunice de Souza, one of India's finest modern poets writes

This time the mountains
were hidden by mist.

My lover is like smoke
my dearest friend far away

And another contemporary poet, Mamang Dai, from Arunachal Pradesh, where the monsoon persists for six months of the year, explores the same metaphors and emotions.

The morning breeze is happy
Releasing drops of water
Whispering, the journey is not over.
Don't ache for love.
Someone will find the lost words.
Grow bamboo and yellow rose,
I'll find you again when I return.

Nainsukh, whose name translates as 'contented eyes', was an eighteenth-century court painter in the Punjab hill state of Guler. Known for his miniature paintings, he conveyed far more than palace scenery or significant events in his patrons' lives. Nainsukh's work explores the aesthetics and moods of classical traditions as interpreted and handed down from earlier generations of poets, musicians, and artists. His *Ragamala* series, 'a garland of melodies', depicts the tones, colours, and textures of musical forms through visual imagery, including human or divine characters that personify each raga. In a miniature entitled *Ragini Madhumadhavi*, he movingly yet simply portrays a young woman shielding herself from the rain as she hurries to take shelter in a pavilion where a bed has been prepared for her and her lover.

The sky is dark with turbulent monsoon clouds and Nainsukh traces gold patterns of serpentine lightning that writhe in the storm. As the eminent art historian B. N. Goswamy describes, 'There is passion in the air and a sense of longing...a young maiden rushes towards a chamber, looking back over her shoulder, one hand holding up a delicately patterned, gold-edged dupatta.... As rain descends in a fine sheet of water in the background and thunder fills the air, thoughts of the lover from whom she is separated in this season of renewal and of union clearly course through her mind.'

The courtiers and aesthetes of Guler, or any other princely state in North India, would have been familiar with the tale of Madhumadhavi, a young woman who braves the threatening darkness of a monsoon storm to meet her lover in secret. Nainsukh's genius lies in the way he illustrates this romantic story and its associated emotions with deft and subtle brushstrokes. A nervous sense of urgency is revealed in the woman's expression and animated stance that contrasts with the still presence of a flowering banana tree in the garden behind her. Rather than showing us the reunion, the beloved's absence in the painting makes the young woman's feelings all the more poignant.

The word 'tryst' has become a cliché in Indian English, and yet its archaic lyricism captures the essence of romantic liaisons in countless monsoon miniatures. Whether it is Radha and Krishna embracing in a leafy bower, or a young princess seated on a swing waiting for her prince to arrive, along with the first rain showers, the anxieties and desires of youthful lovers are distilled in these furtive encounters.

Of all the compositions in Hindustani musical tradition, the raga most closely associated with the monsoon is Megh Malhar. Its name refers to clouds and when it is sung, the arrangement of musical notes invokes the monsoon. Some say that it even causes rain to fall. A popular story associated with this raga recalls how the legendary musician Tansen, in the Mughal emperor Akbar's court, once sang raga Deepak, which generated so much heat in his body that he suffered for days, unable to quench the inner fires aroused by his performance. Eventually, a pair of sisters, Tana and Riri, sang Megh Malhar for him, which cooled the burning in Tansen's body and soul.

The aesthetics of Indian art, literature, and music blur the lines between art forms and genres as well as physical and emotional boundaries. Different artists who celebrate the arrival of the monsoon, whether it be through poetry, painting, or song, employ abstract concepts of carefully classified rasas, or aesthetic qualities, but also arouse a more immediate and visceral awareness of pleasure and pain.

In a more contemporary medium and context, Hindi cinema merges the visual artistry of motion pictures with poetry, song, dance, and drama. One of the most popular Bollywood motifs is the monsoon, which is used both metaphorically and as a narrative device. As film scholar Rachel Dwyer explains, '"Rain songs" in Hindi cinema—film songs in which the rain itself is a character in both the song and its picturization—are usually more specifically associated with eroticism and fertility, and the famous "wet sari" sequence.'

Perhaps the most celebrated monsoon love song in Hindi cinema is 'Pyar Hua Iqrar Hua' (To fall in love is to make a promise) from the 1955 film *Shree 420* starring Raj Kapoor and

Nargis. The lyrics suggest a certain ambivalence despite the insistence on fidelity in the first line, which is followed by 'Pyar se phir kyun dartaa hai dil?' (Then why is the heart afraid of love?) The black and white imagery of rain-swept city streets and the umbrella which the lovers share conjures up nostalgic and romantic notions of the monsoon, in which Raj Kapoor and Nargis wander, knowing they will soon have to part.

## 7

# THE RENEWAL OF LIFE

Returning to Mussoorie in mid-July, after a month in Goa, I find the Landour hillside completely transformed. Oak and deodar trees surrounding our house are draped with ferns and polypods hanging from branches like a fringe of bright green tassels. At 2,500 metres above sea level, the mountains are enveloped in clouds, dense mist drifting through the trees. Stone retaining walls and gate posts are covered in moss and liverworts, giving the rocks a variety of verdant hues. The forest floor, which was carpeted with dry oak leaves in early June, is now hidden beneath a riot of monsoon foliage—wild ginger, strobilanthes, pink and yellow balsam, stinging nettles, and ringal bamboo. Several weeks of rain have brought a multitude of floral species back to life. Hot pink thunder lilies, which emerge at the beginning of the monsoon, are still in bloom. Toothy leaves of wild begonias shield demure blossoms, the size and colour of a child's fingernail.

More than anything, this is a season of botanical resurgence, when the constant rain and mist coax life out of every surface, from tree bark and leaf mulch to brick and concrete. Ancient bryophytes, non-vascular plants which evolved out of aquatic algae and moved onto land roughly 470 million years ago, were the direct ancestors of today's mosses and liverworts. These primitive species do not yield flowers or seeds but reproduce through spores. Ferns are also some of the earliest plants, which appeared on earth 360 million years ago. They too produce spores but possess a vascular system that pumps water and nutrients from their roots to their fronds. Flowering plants, or angiosperms, evolved much later, about 130 million years ago.

The monsoon in Landour transports

us far back in time to the Ordovician and Devonian periods of the Palaeozoic era, when bryophytes and ferns first colonized our planet. This moist, warm climate sustains a range of species that existed on earth long before the age of dinosaurs. At this time of year, we can experience something close to the genesis of terrestrial life. If we study mosses under a magnifying glass, they look like primordial forests in miniature, tiny jungles of cladoxylopsids and *Archaeopteris*, the predecessors of today's trees. On the pushta walls several different species of moss grow together in patches like a variegated mosaic. Liverworts fill in the spaces between, their flat, thin shapes like green scales. Growing out of crevices in the walls are common lip, maidenhair, and nail ferns, each of which have their own feathery shapes and textures. The abundance of greenery suggests an irrepressible creative force that lies dormant for most of the year but erupts with the arrival of the rains, as if through spontaneous generation.

Seeing so many plants sharing the same space—sometimes growing one upon the other, or in and around each other's roots—one cannot help but think of them as a diverse yet integrated community. Whether they are mosses, ferns, flowering plants, or trees, these varied species compete and collaborate with each other, processing light, air, nutrients, and moisture in order to grow and survive. Though we may think of plants as lesser life forms—derisively referring to them as 'biomass', 'weeds', or 'fodder'—they are in fact a richly evolved kingdom of nature. American writer, Paul Hawken, in his provocative book, *Carbon: The Book of Life,* celebrates the intricate complexity of botanical species.

> Plants have developed remarkable methods to know what is happening around them. Bacteria contain about one thousand genes, and fungi ten thousand. Humans have about the same number as mice, twenty-five

thousand genes. Flowering plants can have up to four hundred thousand gene expressions. That doesn't make plants more intelligent but underscores the cumulative complexity that evolved over 470 million years. Because they are immobile, plants sense their surroundings in novel ways. Leaves, stems, and needles are covered with sophisticated networks of interconnected photoreceptors that adjust to capture different wavelengths of light… When attacked by insects, plants emit volatile compounds that other plants detect by smell and taste. Plants have a hygrometer—the ability of roots to detect and precisely measure soil moisture levels. They respond to tactile cues, allowing roots and vines to wend through obstacles. Plant roots dowse for distant sources of water and direct their growth accordingly. They have a perfect nose

> for belowground nutrients, including nitrogen, phosphorus, calcium, and trace minerals… When a specific mineral is needed, plants send specific chemical signals to fungi and bacteria that release minerals from sand or rock enzymatically.

The prolific presence of plants during the monsoon influences us in multiple ways. We are aware of their colours and fragrances, as well as their thorns and bristles. Stinging nettle irritates and inflames our skin while a poultice of crushed dock weed can soothe the itching. Through trial and error, human beings have developed a knowledge of which plants can be used as herbs, for medicines or spices. But more than this, we respond to plants on a psychological or subliminal level, calmed by their leafy companionship, seduced by their tendrils and sinuous forms, inspired by their passivity and persistence. After all, these are species much older than our own, reaching back to a time that we can only imagine—when vegetation ruled the earth.

Another realm of nature that bursts forth during the monsoon is fungi. The mushrooms we see, emerging from the ground or sprouting on tree trunks and branches, are the fruiting bodies of each species, which appear for only a brief period of time and reproduce by casting their spores. Much of the year fungi live unobtrusively out of sight, often in the humus or topsoil of the forest floor, as a network of mycorrhizal hyphae that spreads in all directions. Woven into the living fabric of plant and tree roots, these immeasurably thin strands of mycelium are like a web of delicate embroidery though they firmly stitch together different forms of life.

Until less than two decades ago, fungi were classified as plants, but in 2007 mycologists were able to persuasively argue that these enigmatic organisms should occupy their own kingdom.

Taxonomists also recognized that in some ways fungi have a closer affinity to Animalia than Plantae. At the same time, fungi establish complex and varied relationships with botanical species. Merlin Sheldrake, in his popular book on mycology, *Entangled Life,* explains that fungi were responsible for bringing plants out of the water and on to land, hundreds of millions of years ago, by providing them with root systems before they developed their own. Even today, entwined plant roots and fungal hyphae continue to support each other by exchanging nutrients like phosphorus and communicating through chemical signals.

As Sheldrake writes, 'For as long as fungi have existed, they have been bringing about a "change from the roots". Humans are latecomers to the story. Over hundreds of millions of years, many organisms have formed radical partnerships with fungi. Many—such as plants' relationship with mycorrhizal fungi—have been blockbuster moments in the history of life, with world-changing consequences.'

To study ancient climatic conditions and how these have evolved over time, meteorologists and other scientists have included the presence of mycorrhizal fungi in computer modelling programs that simulate the abundance of plant life aeons ago and estimate the ratio of carbon dioxide and oxygen in the atmosphere. Sheldrake explains how experiments conducted by Katie Field, a biologist at the University of Leeds, indicate that partnerships between plants and fungi could have been responsible for a dramatic episode of global cooling at the end of the Devonian period, 359 million years ago.

> If plants are hitched to an efficient mycorrhizal partner, they receive more phosphorus and grow more. Field was able to estimate how efficient mycorrhizal exchange could have been around 450 million years ago, when atmospheric carbon dioxide levels were several times higher than

> they are today.... The amount of carbon dioxide and oxygen in the atmosphere, and global temperatures—all varied according to the efficiency of mycorrhizal exchange. Based on Field's data, mycorrhizal fungi would have made a substantial contribution to the dramatic drawdown of carbon dioxide that followed the plant boom of the Devonian period....

(Field concluded): 'Our results suggest that mycorrhizal relationships have played a role in the evolution of much of life on Earth.'

During the monsoon in Mussoorie, an array of mushrooms and toadstools appear in the forest. Growing on tree trunks or branches, alongside epiphytic ferns and orchids, we find bleeding oak crust, lacquered brackets, and jelly fungi. Popping out of the ground are giant puffballs, scaly caps, and amethyst deceivers, as well as coral fungi with dozens of finger-like tines. These are edible and when sautéed they have the taste and texture of overcooked scrambled eggs. Tiny mushrooms called parachutes, which grow in fragile clusters, exhibit a lacy beauty while others, like vomiting russula, are as grotesque or repulsive as their names suggest.

Mildew and mould are fungi that follow us indoors. If I go out for a walk in the woods and get caught in the rain, a day or two later my damp shoes will be covered with a powdery green fuzz, as if they've miraculously turned into suede. Wherever there's dampness in the walls or a leak in the roof, black and grey patterns of mould spread like slow-moving maps. Clothes hanging in cupboards during the monsoon acquire the musty odours of various mildews that insinuate their hyphae amongst the woven fibres of wool or cotton. Carpets too are colonized by these fungal intruders that sometimes appear as pale patches on the underside of a rug but are often more evident from the stale, yeasty smell that comes from organic compounds they release into the air.

Being from the kingdom of Animalia, we humans often think of life as something that exists and moves of its own volition, independent of other organisms. In this way, we nurture the conceit that our bodies are insulated or isolated from seemingly inanimate or insentient life forms like plants and fungi, which are rooted to the earth. However, during the monsoon, it is impossible to separate oneself from the profusion of botanical and fungal species that surround us. They brush against you, cling to your hair, and grow between your toes.

This multitude of living colours, scents, flavours, shapes, and textures sustain us in ways that we often forget. Not only do we eat the flowers, fruit, seeds, and leaves of plants, as well as the flesh of mushrooms, but we constantly breathe in spores, pollen, pheromones, and other chemicals that they disperse into the air. At the same time, our bodies host a dynamic population of microbial and mycorrhizal forms of life, especially in our gastrointestinal tract but also in our mouths, sinuses, and lungs, while our skin provides a fertile landscape for microscopic ecosystems. Perhaps someday, just as they did with algae that oozed out of primaeval swamps, fungi will help us put down our own roots.

# 8

# A DANGEROUS SEASON

'Two Mussouns are the Age of a Man', was a gloomy saying in seventeenth- and eighteenth-century British India, when the life expectancy of young colonials was severely curtailed by the number of tropical diseases that flourished during the rains. Whether they contracted malaria or cholera or died of septic wounds that festered in the hot, humid climate, many monsoon ailments were fatal. At that time, one of the most common treatments for various maladies was bloodletting by leeches.

Among the first buildings constructed in Landour was a military sanatorium, where East India Company soldiers and officers were brought to recover from fevers and dysentery. The cooler temperatures and fresh mountain air offered some relief, but many of the patients who came up to the hills did not survive and were soon buried in the Landour Cemetery on the north side of the ridge. Some of the earliest graves date back to the 1830s containing victims of waterborne diseases like typhoid and hepatitis or infections that led to gangrene. Today the old graveyard lies largely neglected. During the monsoon it is overgrown with ferns and stinging nettles, while some of the terraces containing graves have collapsed. Pale shades of mist, like lingering ghosts, drift through the cypress and deodar trees. Only the leeches remain, waiting for warm blooded visitors to wander amongst the forgotten tombs.

Despite its romantic and poetic associations, the monsoon has always been an unhealthy season for human beings and it was generally considered the most malignant time of the year. India's traditional medical systems have recognized the unique illnesses and health risks that exist during the 'varsha ritu' or season of rains. Ayurvedic practitioners classify the three doshas, or bodily humours that sustain life, as vata (wind), kapha (phlegm), and pittam (bile). When these are in balance, a person remains strong and healthy, but when the humours are 'deranged', or thrown out of balance, we grow sick and weaken. The months of Shravan and Bhadra were seen as a time of year when excessive rain and humidity cause an imbalance. The sage Sushrutha, India's first surgeon and the father of Ayurvedic practice, has commented that the excessive moisture and murky qualities of water during the monsoon, as well as the rampant growth of vegetation, weakens both the plants and those who feed on them.

> Oshadhis (Medical plants and cereals) sprout during the rains and are enfeebled in their properties. Water becomes muddy or turbid and the earth is covered over with fresh deposits of washed off or silted mud. The sky becomes overcast with clouds, and the wind, charged with an excess of humidity, dulls the appetite and

> organisms of beings. Hence the food of beings which principally consists of tender and new-grown vegetables of feeble potency, considerably vitiated by the turbid water partaken of as drink during the season, proves acid in its digestive reaction and germinates excessive bile in the human system.

To help maintain health and well-being during the monsoon, specific yoga asanas are prescribed at this season of the year. These vary according to the traditions and teachers. We are told that the Bhujangasana or cobra pose, Naukasana or boat pose, and Setu Bandasana or bridge pose should be performed during the monsoon to boost immunity from diseases and reduce the physical and mental lethargy that accompanies the rain.

Unani medicine, which came to India in the twelfth century CE through Muslim conquest, was patronized by the early sultans of Delhi, as well as rulers in the Deccan.

Later, the Mughal emperors also sponsored Unani hakims or physicians in their courts. Their therapies were based on ancient Greek medical texts, from the time of Hippocrates, which had been translated into Arabic. Unani practitioners believed that everything in nature, including the human body, was composed of four elements—earth, fire, wind, and water. One of the primary precepts was a division of these elements into hot and cold attributes. The Greek calendar was divided into three seasons—winter, summer, and autumn—each of which had its own risks to health and a corresponding regimen of treatments. However, when Graeco–Islamic medicine came to South Asia, it had to adapt to India's six seasons, which included two months of the 'mausam barsaat' or monsoon. Malaria and cholera were unfamiliar diseases for Unani hakims who began to incorporate certain Ayurvedic diagnoses and herbs for their treatment.

The concept of miasmas or polluted air, which caused infections, was one of the guiding principles of Unani medicine and it is easy to imagine how the humid breezes and sultry air of the monsoon might have been considered toxic. The scholar Claudia Prekel refers to a Unani guide to hygiene, *Hadi as-Sihhat,* published in Urdu in 1890 by an assistant-surgeon named Beli Ram. As she explains, 'Two chapters of the *Hadi as-Sihhat* are on the atmospheric air and on the change of seasons.... Ram described the change of the seasons from cold to warm and back to cold. These changes were responsible for diseases.... The *Hadi as-Sihhat* thus underlines the negative effects of the rainy season and describes a scenario of decay and contagion, leading to disease and a high death toll during the monsoon, making it the most dangerous of all seasons.'

One of the Unani prescriptions recommended for maintaining health during the monsoon and promoting proper digestion, was a herbal tonic of fourteen ingredients including pomegranate seeds, cardamom, mint, lemon juice, and a generous dose of tamarind pulp. Known as

Jawarish Tamar Hindi, this decoction was consumed twice a day to help balance the bodily humours during the monsoon.

With the arrival of modern allopathic medicine, particularly antibiotics and anti-malarial drugs, the monsoon is no longer a dreaded time of year. Pesticides have also eradicated many of the mosquitoes that flourished with the rain. Nevertheless, Ayurvedic and Unani therapies are still popular options for individuals who suffer from lassitude, gastrointestinal ailments, and skin diseases during the monsoon. Certain insect-borne fevers like dengue and chikungunya remain a serious threat, particularly as the rain tapers off in late August and September.

The monsoon brings other kinds of suffering too. Powerful storms during May 2025, led to mudslides and flash floods across the lower Himalaya. Villages and towns in Uttarakhand, Himachal Pradesh, and Kashmir were inundated by a deluge of water and debris that washed away or buried houses in the mountains.

Directly to the north of us in Mussoorie lies the watershed of the Ganga where the annual Char Dham Yatra attracts hundreds of thousands of pilgrims to Yamunotri, Gangotri, Kedarnath, and Badrinath near the sources of the sacred river. This region is also a popular destination for trekkers. To accommodate the yearly influx of devotees and tourists, an ever-increasing number of hotels, homestays, resorts, ashrams, and restaurants have been built along the course of the Ganga's major tributaries. With a scarcity of level ground, many of these structures are erected on land that lies in the path of flash floods.

In 2013, a catastrophic natural disaster struck Kedarnath and the Mandakini Valley, when a glacial lake outburst, triggered by excessive rain, sent an enormous wave of water, mud, and rocks through the temple town and on downstream as far as Rishikesh and

Haridwar. The devastation was horrific and countless pilgrims and villagers lost their lives while hotels, homes, and fields were wiped out in an instant by the flash flood. This was a warning to those who had constructed buildings at sites that were vulnerable to monsoon torrents. However, as the number of pilgrims and trekkers increases every year, the obvious dangers continue to be ignored.

At 1.30 p.m. on Tuesday, 5 August 2025, the residents of Dharali, a village 25 kilometres below Gangotri on the Bhagirathi branch of the Ganga, were preparing to celebrate an annual festival in honour of a local deity. Suddenly, a loud explosion was heard from the valley above, where the Kheerganga, a small tributary of the Bhagirathi, flows out of the mountains and through Dharali. Seconds later, a huge flood of water came pouring down on the town, destroying the main market as well as many guest houses and other facilities for trekkers and pilgrims. An alluvial fan of sludge and rubble covered everything in its path. More than seventy people lost their lives.

This flood was probably caused by a glacial lake outburst high above the village or a landslide that blocked the Kheerganga and then suddenly burst. The Himalaya, which are some of the youngest mountains on earth, are a geologically unstable region. Settlements like Dharali are vulnerable to the unpredictable forces of hydrology, erosion, and earthquakes. Monsoon storms loosen the soil and wash quantities of moraine and other loose debris down narrow valleys, often with devastating results.

This is not the first time that a disaster like this has occurred near Dharali. In 2013 and 2011, similar catastrophes struck the Assi Ganga Valley, further downstream near Uttarkashi. And way back in 1880, a major flash flood inundated the upper Bhagirathi Valley below Gangotri. Frederick Wilson, a rapacious timber baron who clear-felled most of the deodar trees near Dharali, had built himself a palatial home in Harsil, 2 kilometres below the village.

Known as Raja Wilson, he ruled the valley and minted his own coins. When the flood occurred, newspapers reported that Wilson had been washed away and drowned. However, as preparations were underway for a memorial service in Mussoorie, Wilson suddenly appeared, having miraculously survived the flood.

This proves that the tragic consequences of a heavy monsoon in populated areas of the Himalaya is not something new or unexpected. What has changed is the unplanned and often illegal construction of guest houses, trekking lodges, yoga retreats, and other facilities for pilgrims or tourists that lie directly in the path of potential flash floods. While the region surrounding Dharali has been designated as an 'eco-sensitive zone' and government regulations restrict unauthorized construction, political opportunism and administrative apathy allow villagers and outsiders to take desperate risks.

## 9

## BEETLE HUNTING

When I was a boy, growing up in Landour, the monsoon was a time for collecting things, particularly beetles and other bugs. The rains brought with them a vast assortment of crawling creatures like the common house spiders that appeared on our bedroom walls, sometimes bearing white silk egg sacs full of dozens of tiny spiderlings that scattered in all directions if the sac broke. Though the adult spiders looked alarmingly large, these were harmless creatures that helped control insect pests. Another arachnid that often appeared indoors during the monsoon were scorpions that squeezed through gaps under the doors or crept in by way of bathroom drains. They sometimes took refuge in our shoes and every morning we made a habit of knocking the heels of our sneakers together and shaking them vigorously to make sure that nothing was hiding inside.

As budding naturalists, beetles were our prime objective, and best collected near the streetlights on the Chakkar and Tehri roads. As soon as it grew dark, we would set out with our gumboots and umbrellas, as well as long bamboo poles, with which we knocked beetles off the lamp posts and nearby trees. They would often buzz through the air like incoming drones while our torch beams pierced the darkness as if they were searchlights.

Hundreds of species of beetles emerged in the monsoon but there were a dozen or so that we hunted, and for these we had our own names. The largest were 'common stags', with pincers that looked like antlers, 3 to 5 centimetres long. Females of this species were called 'cows' and had small, sharp pincers like nail clippers that delivered a painful bite. Another kind of stag beetle was a glossier black and somewhat smaller. These were dubbed 'Chinese stags' for reasons I can't explain. 'Bamboo beetles' used to be the most common species, a bit like large cockroaches with rusty-red bodies and long antennae. Difficult to hold between your thumb and forefinger because of a soft carapace, they squirmed wildly when you picked them up. The pincers on bamboo beetles were compact and strong, effortlessly snapping through matchsticks and twigs. Alongside these were several species of rhinoceros beetles. The most common were 'cherry rhinos', which had three horns instead of pincers. They appeared black at night but in daylight their wing plates had a rich, reddish hue. When we picked them up, they made a chirring sound that we interpreted as angry cursing, which is why we called them 'swear beetles'. Of all the Mussoorie Coleoptera the rarest and most prized were 'five-horned rhinos' that were bigger than golf balls with orange and black markings. Aside from these we caught 'sawtooths' and 'stone carriers', both a speckled grey colour. The former had serrated pincers from which they got their name while the latter had long antennae that stretched backwards like the trump line or head straps used by Nepali labourers in Mussoorie.

In recent years, many of us have noticed that fewer and fewer beetles are found in Landour and a variety of theories have been put forward to explain their diminishing numbers. Some experts suggest that there is less dead wood in the forests. Many beetles lay their eggs in rotting branches or under dry, desiccated bark. Another explanation is that an increasing number of forest fires have destroyed their habitat. As a result of climate change, rising temperatures and reduced humidity could also have affected the beetle population. But no entomologists that I'm aware of have applied themselves to the problem and without a careful survey of species it's impossible to gauge exactly what has happened. All I know is that the whirring of beetles' wings is no longer a common sound on monsoon nights.

During mid-August 2025, I was able to team up with Vivek Sarkar, a senior project scientist at the Wildlife Institute of India (WII) in Dehradun. An authority on cicadas and other insects, Vivek joined me in Landour for four days to film a short video about biodiversity during the monsoon. Our objective was simple—to find and document as many creatures as we could locate during this short space of time. Though heavy rain often interrupted our foraging, we came upon a remarkable range of life forms that Vivek and I were able to capture in videos and still photographs.

August is the liveliest month of the monsoon when insects are most active. In preparation for Vivek's visit, I took several short recces around the hillside before he arrived. Walking down a trail that leads from our house to a campsite known as Fairy Glen, I scanned the fern-laden trees as well as the wet leaves littering the ground for any signs of life. Passing a moss-covered oak, I spotted a small black object about the size of a pinhead. When I peered under the layered fringe of ferns, I could just make out the shape of a cicada hiding in the shadows. About as long as my index finger, it was perfectly camouflaged. The black spot was one of its eyes, while the mottled colouration on its head and body matched the green shades and textures of the moss. Its wings were transparent, except for a latticework of black veins. The cicada sat perfectly still while I photographed it, but when I looked up from the camera's viewfinder, it seemed to disappear because it blended into its surroundings so completely, like an optical illusion.

Later, when he arrived, Vivek identified this species as *Platylomia brevis*, the most common cicada found in Landour at this time of year. These arboreal insects call for about an hour at dusk, a persistent sound between a whine and a rattle. Vivek explained that the ratcheting cry is made by the male to attract its mate, who remains silent. Male cicadas have a specific organ, known as a tymbal, that produces the sound. They also have two membrane-like appendages that cover the tymbal and help amplify the sound, as do the hollow cavities in their abdomens. The twilight hour when cicadas call is precisely timed to avoid predators. Males begin their tymbalation after most birds have settled down for the night and they stop calling as soon as bats begin flying about in the dark.

Vivek's interest in entomology began when he was a child growing up in Siliguri and other parts of West Bengal, where he would often hear cicadas calling. Pursuing these elusive creatures led him to a career in wildlife science that has extended over more than twenty years. He explains how the cicadas he heard as a child are a species that were formerly known only in Thailand, though his research established that they are distributed as far west as the foothills below Darjeeling.

In our quest for monsoon species, we come upon a variety of caterpillars, most of which are moth larvae. One of these has a unique defensive strategy to protect itself from birds.

After hatching, the caterpillars swarm together in dense clusters on the ground. A ruddy brown colour, they look like splotches of cow dung from a distance, though on closer inspection we discover a writhing mass of worms. Birds are fooled into thinking these are a single, larger creature that looks decidedly unappetizing.

Turning over a stone, I find a semi-slug, which is one of the oddest gastropods on earth. In the middle of its back, partly covered by a fleshy flap of skin, is what looks like a half-formed shell. This gives semi-slugs the appearance of being some kind of mutation or partially evolved species though taxonomists have identified them as a separate family of invertebrates. We also found several hammerhead slugs, which have slick black bodies, about 5 to 8 centimetres long, and a club-like head that protrudes on either side. Snails are also common in the monsoon and come in different sizes, from the diameter of a pomegranate seed to some that are larger than chestnuts with ornate amber shells. One of the creatures I didn't see, until I returned home, were leeches that had inched their way up my shoes and fastened themselves to my ankles.

Before dark on the first evening, we set up a mercury vapour lamp. Behind the bare, oversized bulb, Vivek draped a plain white sheet. Soon enough, scores of moths and other insects, including cicadas and beetles, were attracted to the light and the cotton cloth became a living tapestry embroidered with wings of different shapes, textures, and colours. As Vivek photographed each species, more and more moths arrived, along with a few opportunistic bats that swooped in to snatch an easy meal. During his four days in Landour, checking the lamp at all hours of the night, Vivek was able to document more than eighty different species of moths.

At dawn each morning, birds arrived to feast on this banquet of Lepidoptera. A family of blue whistling thrushes, including two fledglings, was the most aggressive, eagerly pecking at the insects and swallowing them, wings and all. Also in attendance were a pair of grey-winged blackbirds, as well as streaked laughingthrushes that gleaned the few moths that the others had left behind.

Many other insects were also attracted to the light. A couple of cicadas put in an appearance as did a female cherry rhino and several emerald June bugs. One of the strangest creatures was a Dobson fly, about 7 centimetres long, most of which consisted of its pale, yellow wings and an extended neck and head with lethal jaws that make it look like a miniature dragon. A variety of parasitic wasps also clung to the white sheet. Some of the females were equipped with long, flexible appendages that look like stingers, though they are harmless to humans. These ovipositors are used to lay wasp eggs inside the larvae or pupae of other insects or on the outside of their bodies. When the wasp larvae hatch, they feed off the host. Vivek informed me that many caterpillars are covered in bristling hairs to defend themselves from parasitic wasps.

Knowing that we were unlikely to find many beetles during Vivek's short visit, I had asked our gardener, Govind Ram, to collect some from the lamp post near his home at Jabarkhet, half a kilometre below Oakville. For reasons I initially couldn't understand, Govind had told me that quite a few beetles were attracted to this particular street lamp but not to other lights along the road. Before Vivek's arrival, Govind was able to collect about a dozen 'cows' and 'cherry rhinos' as well as one handsome 'Chinese stag', 8 centimetres long. These were kept in glass bottles with holes punched in the lids. Remembering how I'd fed them when I was boy, I put slices of ripe mango in the bottles. The beetles gorged on the fruit, which quickly began to ferment, emitting a strong odour that immediately took me back to my days as a juvenile coleopterist.

Vivek and I spent several hours filming the beetles, placing them in locations like the rotting trunk of a Himalayan maple in our yard, its bark covered with lichens. Two years ago, I'd spotted a common stag on this tree. A friend of Vivek's who specializes in beetles had told him that certain species of Coleoptera feed on lichens. Perhaps under the influence of fermented mango juice, the beetles were more than cooperative. After we finished filming, we released them in the dark and I felt a certain nostalgia as a couple of them flew off on buzzing wings.

As we experimented with the moth light, it became clear that the mercury vapour bulb, with its bright yellow aura, was most effective in attracting night-flying insects. When I replaced it with an energy-efficient LED bulb, this attracted no more than two or three moths, though the illumination was considerably stronger. As Vivek explained, insects are attracted to shorter wavelengths of light, particularly UV rays emitted by old fashioned light bulbs like the mercury vapour lamp. LED bulbs, which give off a cool white glow, are least likely to attract moths and beetles. When we checked the lamp post near Govind's home, we found it was fitted with a traditional bulb that emitted a warm yellow aura.

Suddenly, I had at least part of an answer to the disappearance of beetles in Landour. Though their numbers have clearly declined, probably because of changes in the climate and other environmental factors, it is also obvious that we're not seeing them as frequently as we did because most of the lamp posts in Landour are now fitted with LED bulbs. In this way, our perceptions of changes in the natural world are sometimes unintentionally a result of the technology we employ. Whatever it may be, I was relieved that the beetles hadn't suffered a mass extinction as I'd feared. Hearing the buzz of their wings and seeing them whizzing through the drizzle and mist, I felt as if monsoon nights in Landour were not as empty or silent as I'd thought.

Part of our fascination with insects and other invertebrates that emerge during the monsoon comes from their diminutive size. When we observe them closely, they reduce us to their scale while magnifying the world they inhabit. The tiny flies and worms that clamber up a stem of spikemoss and other lycophytes sprouting from a pushta wall are virtually inaccessible to us, though we can see them with our naked eyes if we lean down to their level or view them through a camera lens. To watch a snail, a caterpillar, or a beetle in its natural habitat is to see a creature that dominates this miniature wilderness just as elephants, tigers, and other megafauna assert their presence in a jungle. These intimate green realms, which we might otherwise overlook, captivate our imaginations with their complex synchronicities, where a drop of rainwater suspended from the tip of a fern is twice as large as the crab spider that crouches patiently on the same frond, waiting to make a meal of a microscopic insect, one tenth its size. These infinitesimal ecosystems are as richly populated and diverse as the forest of oaks and deodars that tower above us.

We usually think of the monsoon on a much greater and grander scale, with massive cloud formations, powerful storms, devastating floods, and tempestuous winds—the kind of weather that makes us feel insignificant and dwarfed by the magnitude of nature's forces. Yet, this same volatile climate extends down to the most intricate forms of life, which can survive and flourish in a deluge, where the monsoon nurtures the tiniest animals, fungi, plants, and bacteria. Here in these delicate yet resilient landscapes, the rain means as much to those minuscule species as it does to us.

## 10

# THE WAYWARD WANDERER

The end of the monsoon is often as inconclusive and enigmatic as its beginnings. Some of the worst storms in the Himalaya strike in the final weeks of August, just when it seems as if the rains are on their way out. In 2025, heavy downpours and flooding occurred in Uttarakhand at the start of September, causing numerous landslides and collapsed roads. Two of the main arteries of the Char Dham Yatra, to Gangotri and Yamunotri, were blocked and the state government took the unprecedented decision to suspend part of the annual pilgrimage because of safety concerns. Even northern Ladakh was hit by rainstorms and mudslides, while areas of western Kashmir occupied by Pakistan were badly affected by flash floods, proving that the monsoon does not respect ceasefire lines or borders.

In Mussoorie, we often say that 15 September is the last day of the rains but on the morning of 16 September 2025, when it seemed that the worst of the storms were over, a sudden cloudburst struck Mussoorie and Dehradun, dropping as much as 195 millimetres (7.5 inches) of rain within a period of twelve hours. This caused enormous destruction, killing at least fifteen people, and leaving hundreds homeless. Bridges were washed away, houses collapsed, and roads were buried beneath a slurry of debris that spewed out of narrow ravines and small streams, which had turned into rivers. Housing colonies built along watercourses were swept away. The main motor road to Mussoorie, as well as all of the other access routes were blocked by damaged bridges or landslides. Thousands of tourists were stranded in the hill station, and it took more than two days before traffic was restored, after the roads were finally cleared and the army constructed temporary bridges. The destruction has been estimated to cost hundreds of crores of rupees. In this way, just as the rains began with devastating storms, they ended with a disturbing reminder of nature's fury.

In Landour, which suffered less damage than neighbouring areas, the first sign of the monsoon coming to a close are the ferns turning brown. Epiphytic species depend on the enveloping mist as much as the rain to keep their roots damp while they cling to tree bark. As soon as the humidity starts to drop, along with evening temperatures, the green beards of moss and polypods that sprout from oak and deodar branches begin to wither and turn a rusty tan.

You can often feel a change in the air, even before the wet weather subsides, a hint of autumn in the evening breezes that sweep aside the clouds at sunset. While most of the foliage remains green for another month, many of the flowers—balsam and wild ginger, as well as ground orchids—begin to disappear, as do the mushrooms. Moths and other insects reach the end of this stage in their life cycles and start to vanish. Even the leeches depart and by the middle of September, a walk in the woods no longer carries the risk of bloodied ankles, even if the rain still falls occasionally. October is the month that all of us wait for in Mussoorie, when we can finally step outdoors without the fear of getting drenched. At last, we can put away our umbrellas, raincoats, and gumboots.

After living in the clouds for three months, there is a sense of relief when the air eventually clears, and we can see further than the edge of our yard. The views surprise us, though we've seen them many times before. Looking southwards, beyond the urban sprawl of Dehradun and the forested Shivalik Range, the Doab stretches to the horizon in a patchwork of fields and villages. To the west, we can see the Yamuna and to the east, the Ganga, both rivers running high, reflecting the evening sunlight like veins of gold. The sky has been washed clean of dust and pollution. To the north of Landour, the high Himalaya—freshly covered with snow—stand out clear and crisp, after having been hidden since June. All at once our whole perspective changes as distant landmarks, ridgelines, and valleys become visible. The claustrophobic closeness of the mist no longer holds us in its grasp and the surrounding trees come into focus, instead of being blurred by moving clouds.

The departure of the monsoon reminds us that this is a seasonal journey, the annual migration of air and moisture. While we remained safe at home, listening to the reassuring sound of rain on the roof, those winds and water vapours were constantly in motion, traversing the sky, circling and dispersing, rising and falling. This itinerant climate is a wayward wanderer that takes its leave before we know it and goes back to the sea, from whence it came.

# ACKNOWLEDGEMENTS

We are grateful to Andrew Schelling for granting permission to reprint his translation of Vidya's untitled poem as an epigraph in this book. This translation was first published in *Vidya: Old Time Love Song Magic* by Circumference Books, New York, 2025.

# NOTES

**p. 7 'In 1964...blood of the gods':** I. J. Bear and R. G. Thomas, 'The Nature of Argillaceous Odour', *Nature,* Vol. 201, No. 4923, 7 March 1964, pp. 993–95.

**p. 9 'carried uphill on anabatic winds...key climatic feature of the Himalayan Foothills':** S. C. Bose, *Geography of the Himalaya*, New Delhi: National Book Trust, 1972, pp. 48–49.

**p. 10 'active Madden–Julian...Indian Ocean':** Nayonika Bose, 'As early monsoon hits Mumbai, the key factor: Madden-Julian Oscillation', *Indian Express*, 26 May 2025.

**p. 13 'The southwest monsoon...on May 23':** Anjali, Marar, 'What Monsoon "onset" means, why it is early', *Indian Express*, 26 May 2025.

**p. 13 'The India Meteorological...were favourable':** Alind Chauhan, 'The history and evolution of monsoon forecasting in India', *Indian* Express, 27 May 2025.

**p. 15 'The monsoon seemed...life very complicated':** Alexander Frater, *Chasing the Monsoon,* London: Picador, 1990, pp. 53–54.

**p. 15 'The imbroglio...down to the sea':** Ibid., p. 60.

**p. 18 'a South American species...aboard Spanish galleons':** Pradip Krishen, *Trees of Delhi*, New Delhi: Dorling Kindersley, 2006, p. 282.

**p. 21 'There was once...in the nineteenth century':** Benjamin J. Israel, *The Jews of India*, New Delhi: Mosaic Books, 1982, p. 9.

**p. 32 'Right from the eighteenth...across the known world':** Vivek Menezes, 'Goan Mangoes are the Best in the World – History Proves So, Too', *Scroll.in*, 25 May 2017.

**p. 44 'the advent of the monsoon...forces of good and evil':** Sushil Mittal and Gene Thursby (eds.), *Hindu World: An Encyclopedic Survey of Hinduism*, New Delhi: Routledge, 2004, p. 92.

**p. 51 'In 1991...monsoon wind strength':** Peter D. Clift and R. Alan Plumb, *The Asian Monsoon: Causes, History and Effects*, New York: Cambridge University Press, 2008, p. 51.

**p. 54 'The name, "monsoon"...into English usage':** Henry Yule and A. C. Burnell, *Hobson-Jobson: A Glossary of Colloquial Anglo-Indian Words and Phrases, and of Kindred Terms Etymological, Historical, Geographical and Discursive*, William Crooke (ed.), New Delhi: Motilal Banarsidass Publishing House, 2011, p. 577.

**p. 76 'Thunderclouds...Expecting him':** Arvind Krishna Mehrotra, *The Absent Traveller*, New Delhi: Penguin Books, 2008, p. 57.

**p. 76 'Metaphors take longer...own literatures':** Ibid., p. x.

**p. 77 'The rainy season...where he is?':** M. L. Thangappa (tr.), *Love Stands Alone: Selections from Tamil Sangam Poetry*, New Delhi: Penguin Random House, 2020, p. 29.

**p. 78 'Their rocks caressed...moods of longing':** A. N. D. Haksar (tr.), *Ritusamhara, A Gathering of Seasons*, New Delhi: Penguin Random House, 2018, p. 48.

**p. 80 'The wayward wind...hearts of lonely lovers':** R. S. Pandit (tr.), *Ritusamhara or The Pageant of the Seasons*, Bombay: National Information & Publications, 1947, p. 41.

**p. 80 'The cloud rains…day like this':** Sunil Sharma, '"The Spring of Hindustan": Love and War in the Monsoon in Indo-Persian Poetry', *Monsoon Feelings: A History of Emotions in the Rain*, Imke Rajamani, Katherine Butler Schofield, and Margrit Pernau (eds.), New Delhi: Niyogi Books, 2018, p. 54.

**p. 81 'Now the heavy month…clutched my soul':** Francesca Orsini, 'Clouds, Cuckoos and an Empty Bed. Emotions in Hindi-Urdu Barahmasas', *Monsoon Feelings*, p. 108.

**p. 82 'How does one…counting the stars':** Dihlavi Ghalib, *Divan-i Ghalib Urdu*, New Delhi: Ghalib Academy, 1993, p. 141. Also in Sunil Sharma, 'The Spring of Hindustan…', *Monsoon Feelings*, p. 67.

**p. 82 'Even as...him on course':** Sunil Sharma, 'The Spring of Hindustan…', Monsoon Feelings, p. 67.

**p. 83 'This time the mountains…friend far away':** Eunice de Souza, *A Necklace of Skulls*, New Delhi: Penguin Books, 2009, p. 49.

**p. 83 'The morning…when I return':** Mamang Dai, *The White Shirts of Summer*, New Delhi: Speaking Tiger, 2023, p. 54.

**p. 84 'There is passion...course through her mind':** B. N. Goswamy, *Nainsukh of Guler*, New Delhi: Niyogi Books, 1997, p. 240.

**p. 87 '"Rain songs"..."wet sari" sequence':** Rachel Dwyer, 'Rimjhim ke Taraane Leke Aayi Barsaat: Songs of Love and Longing in the Bombay Rain', *Monsoon Feelings*, p. 293.

**p. 92 'Plants have developed...rock enzymatically':** Paul Hawken, *Carbon: The Book of Life*, New York: Viking, 2025, pp. 90–91.

**p. 96 'Merlin Sheldrakc...developed their own':** Merlin Sheldrake, *Entangled Lives: How Fungi Make our Worlds, Change our Minds, and Shape our Futures*, London: Penguin Books, 2020, p. 4.

**p. 96 'For as long...world-changing consequences':** Ibid., p. 211.

**p. 97 'If plants are hitched...of life on Earth':** Ibid., pp. 146–47.

**p. 98 'During the monsoon...their name suggests':** *Mushrooms and Other Fungi of Jabarkhet Nature Reserve*, Jabarkhet Nature Reserve.

**p. 102 'Two Mussouns are the Age of a Man':** Sir Henry Yule and A. C. Burnell, *Hobson-Jobson: The Definitive Glossary of British India*, Oxford: Oxford University Press, 2013, p. 354.

**p. 104 'Oshadhis…the human system':** Kaviraj Kunja Lal Bhishagratna, *An English Translation of The Sushruta Samhita*, Vol. 1, Calcutta: J. N. Bose, 1907, p. 48.

**p. 105 'To help maintain…accompanies the rain':** 'Try this simple sequence of monsoon yoga for immunity', ArtofLiving.org, available at https://www.artofliving.org/in-en/yoga/yoga-sequences-for/monsoon-yoga-for-immunity.

**p. 107 'Two chapters…dangerous of all seasons':** Claudia Preckel,'"The Most Dangerous Season of All": Monsoon in Unani Medical Writings', *Monsoon Feelings*, pp. 364–65.

**p. 107 'One of the Unani…"Jawarish Tamar Hindi"':** Ibid., pp. 349–50.